Love &
Nurture
in the Early Years

Sara Miller McCune founded Sage Publishing in 1965 to support the dissemination of useable knowledge and educate a global community. Sage publishes more than 1000 journals and over 800 new books each year, spanning a wide range of subject areas. Our growing selection of library products includes archives, data, case studies and video. Sage remains majority owned by our founder and after her lifetime will become owned by a charitable trust that secures the company's continued independence.

Los Angeles | London | New Delhi | Singapore | Washington DC | Melbourne

Aaron Bradbury
Tamsin Grimmer

Love &
Nurture
in the Early Years

Learning Matters
A Sage Publishing Company
1 Oliver's Yard
55 City Road
London EC1Y 1SP

Sage Publications Inc.
2455 Teller Road
Thousand Oaks, California 91320

Sage Publications India Pvt Ltd
B 1/I 1 Mohan Cooperative Industrial Area
Mathura Road
New Delhi 110 044

Sage Publications Asia-Pacific Pte Ltd
3 Church Street
#10-04 Samsung Hub
Singapore 049483

Library of Congress Number Available

British Library Cataloguing in Publication Data

A catalogue record for this book is available from the British Library

Editor: Amy Thornton
Senior project editor: Chris Marke
Project management: TNQ Tech Pvt. Ltd.
Cover design: Wendy Scott
Typeset by: TNQ Tech Pvt. Ltd.
Printed in the UK

ISBN 978-1-5296-7098-1
ISBN 978-1-5296-7097-4 (pbk)

CONTENTS

ABOUT THE AUTHORS

Aaron Bradbury is the Principal Lecturer for Early Years and Childhood and Early Childhood Studies at Nottingham Trent University. Aaron is a Member of the Coalition for the Early Years on the Birth to Five Matters Non-Statutory Guidance for the EYFS and chaired and written the Equalities and Inclusion section with colleagues in the sector.

Aaron is a published author on early childhood theories and child development. He sits on many national early childhood groups and is also a consultant on many aspects of early years and child development. Aaron has spoken as a keynote speaker both nationally and internationally on contemporary issues within the early childhood sector. Aaron has a passion for making the voice of the child, nurturing through a diverse lens and pioneers of early childhood the foreground of practice.

Tamsin Grimmer is a Director of Linden Learning, an associate of Early Education, Principal Lecturer at Norland College and an Emotion Coaching Practitioner for Emotion Coaching UK.

Tamsin has worked in the early years sector all her professional life, as a teacher, EYFS adviser, Area SENCo, Childminder, Assessor and mentor for EYPS/EYTs and as a consultant.

As an advocate for listening to young children, Tamsin supports practitioners to make learning multi-sensory, active and playful. Tamsin has a wealth of experience supporting Early Years Teachers and educators. She is passionate about young children's learning and believes that all children deserve educators who are inspiring, dynamic, reflective and loving. Tamsin is a true advocate for adopting a loving pedagogy and has a keen interest in schematic play, promoting positive behaviour, supporting children's emotional development and inclusion.

Tamsin has written several books aimed at educators and particularly enjoys delivering training and offering consultancy supporting early childhood professionals to improve outcomes for young children.

ACKNOWLEDGEMENTS

We have so many people to thank who have helped to bring this book to life, but want to start with the children. So a big thank you to Charlotte, Finnbar, Harry, Jess, Lola M, Lola S and Max for entering our front cover competition. We loved all your pictures so much that we have included one at the start of each chapter to enable our readers to enjoy them too. An extra well done to Max our cover artist, whose drawing of a teddy depicts love beautifully.

Our thanks go to David Wright for sharing his inspiring opening speech for the World Forum on Early Care and Education; Peter Walker for his insights into baby massage; Wendy Dormer and her teams at Conewood Children's Centre and Westbourne Early Years Centre; Caroline Wright and her team at Bright Horizons; Shana Laffy for her expertise around emotion coaching; Dr Natalie Canning for sharing her empowerment framework; Kate Bate for her case studies about continuous provision and nurturing approach.

In addition, thank you to those educators who have shared their lived experiences and stories about their nurturing ethos and loving pedagogy and enabled us to really see the impact it has on their children. You know who you are!

Final thanks go to our partners and our mums, for your love and nurture!

INTRODUCTION

We, Aaron and Tamsin, have worked together on a number of occasions and discovered that our ethos is aligned in terms of wanting to inspire early childhood professionals to create a loving, nurturing environment for young children. With this in mind, we wanted to write this book together, in the hope that it will inspire others in their work with young children.

We thought it might be helpful to begin with what this book is not. The term 'nurture' is often used in conjunction with the nature–nurture debate. We are not debating this – we see nature and nurture as combined and impossible to separate. In addition, the Center on the Developing Child, Harvard University, outlines that recent neuroscientific developments imply the idea of nature versus nurture is outdated and the study of epigenetics suggests that although our genetic code is embedded at conception, it is through our nurturing environment that children grow and develop (Center on the Developing Child, 2023). Therefore, in terms of child development, we would suggest both nature and nurture are important.

When thinking about nurturing children, this implies caring for them through their development over time, or as they grow. We might nurture curiosity, nurture kindness or nurture creativity in our children, which means we help our children to develop these virtues or foster these dispositions. To nurture someone is to care deeply for them and help them to grow and thrive. In this sense, our early childhood provision is predominantly about nurturing children. This goes hand in hand with loving children. It would be impossible to truly love a child without nurturing them, because real love is active and wants the very best for the other person. Therefore, considering both love and nurture seems a very natural combination.

However, loving and nurturing doesn't come without any risk... in loving others we allow ourselves to become vulnerable and as Bowlby points out, 'A liability to experience separation anxiety and grief are thus the ineluctable risks of a love relationship, of caring for someone' (1960, p. 110). In loving our children as early childhood professionals, we open ourselves to hurt; however, we would argue that loving our children is still the best way, in fact, the only way of nurturing them.

We hope that this book will offer practical advice and guidance about how to love and nurture young children, backed up and embedded by a wealth of theory and research.

ORGANISATION OF BOOK

Within this book, we use the term 'early childhood professional' to mean anyone who is working with young children in a professional context, regardless of their job title or qualification. When we use the term 'parents and carers', we are referring to anyone who has parental responsibility for a child, whether a birth parent, adopted parent, foster parent, grandparent or other individual.

We want our writing to be accessible to everyone regardless of their level of training or qualifications; therefore, we have tried to write as clearly as possible. Each chapter begins with aims as an overview for the reader, followed by definitions of the key terms used within the chapter. The chapter is then introduced and more detailed discussion follows. We have included case studies and examples from practice to exemplify the themes discussed and activities or reflective activities where appropriate. Each chapter has a conclusion, which summarises the points raised. We believe critical reflection to be an important aspect of continuing our own professional journey and, with this in mind, every chapter ends with some key questions. Chapter 8 is organised slightly differently as it summarises the key learning from each chapter and provides links to further reading and resources.

CITIZENS OF TOMORROW

Ultimately, the approach we adopt within our early childhood schools and settings determines what we want for our children and for society in the future. Do we want compliant, obedient children, who do what adults say without thinking for themselves, and thus grow adults who accept the status quo and submit to all authority, regardless of morality? Or do we want to grow and nurture loving citizens of tomorrow who know right from wrong, are capable of making moral choices and are empathetic towards their fellow citizens whilst working towards the common good? Their future is in our hands. How we love and nurture our children today will determine how loving and nurturing they become in the future.

Our friend and colleague David Wright, the National Representative for England for the World Forum on Early Care and Education, opened the World Forum gathering in 2023 with the following words. We found his opening speech really inspiring and wanted to give the last word in this introduction to him, so with permission, we are sharing it now. His vision for early childhood education, that change in the world begins with our youngest children, is what we want to achieve through loving and nurturing them.

Enroute to the World Forum on Early Care and Education (ECE) gathering in Orlando last year (2022), I took the opportunity to visit the Lincoln Memorial in Washington DC. From its top I looked out across the water in front of me and imagined being amongst the crowd on August 28th 1963 hearing Dr Martin Luther King's historic *I have a dream* speech delivered from those iconic steps.

One thing that strikes me about the text of his speech is his focus on the children –

Now is the time to make justice a reality for all of God's **children.**

We can never be satisfied as long as our **children** *are stripped of their selfhood and robbed of their dignity...*

I have a dream that... one day right down in Alabama, **little black boys and black girls** *will be able to join hands with* **little white boys and white girls** *as sisters and brothers.*

Why, I wonder, did he choose to paint a picture of a future world of equity and justice populated by children? I would suggest that he did so deliberately because he recognised that early childhood is where the values of the next generation are formed and where the cycle of intergenerational hatred, discrimination and injustice can all be changed.

I first attended a World Forum conference in Belfast in 2009. The then president of Ireland, Mary McAleese, travelled up from Dublin to address the conference. Her words have remained with me. She told us how a deliberate policy of siting ECE settings on the boundaries of sectarian communities had brought former enemies together for the sake of their children – little catholic boys and girls, joining hands with little protestant boys and girls as sisters and brothers. This is where the peace process was being played out.

And I think of our friend Eddy, the World Forum national representative for Rwanda. Eddy, whose family was butchered by his neighbours during the 1994 genocide, who fled the country but subsequently chose to return and live amongst those who had killed his family. He now establishes and supports ECE settings across Rwanda, to bring reconciliation and hope to broken communities. Little Tutsi boys and girls, joining hands with little Hutu boys and girls as sisters and brothers.

Delegates of the World Forum on Early Care and Education represent organisations working in ECE centres across the World, some in the most impoverished and disadvantaged areas on the planet. I have visited some of these. Without exception, they are hubs of their communities, places of acceptance, restoration and hope.

May we take the opportunity to learn from one another; to celebrate our **differences**; to build our **relationships** and as we consider our individual commitment to ECE in the years ahead, may we return to our own context, carrying with us that same dream and **spirit** in the realisation that the **change** we want to see in the World, starts with our youngest **children** and that we are the ones privileged to make it happen.

This speech really resonated with us because we believe early childhood education to be vital in shaping future society. David's ideas align with our beliefs and ethos around the importance of relationships and how nurture and love really can change the world and bring about a more peaceful society, one child at a time.

References

Bowlby J. (1960) Separation anxiety. *The International Journal of Psycho-Analysis*, 41, pp. 89–113.

Centre on the Developing Child, Harvard University (2023) *Epigenetics and Child Development: How Children's Experiences Affect Their Genes*. Boston, MA: Centre on the Developing Child, Harvard University. Available at: https:// developingchild.harvard.edu/resources/what-is-epigenetics-and-how-does-it-relate-to-child-development/#:~:text=% E2%80%9CEpigenetics%E2%80%9D%20is%20an%20emerging%20area,is%20no%20longer%20a%20debate

Luther King, M. (1963) *Transcript of Speech*. Available at: https://www.archives.gov/files/social-media/transcripts/ transcript-march-pt3-of-3-2602934.pdf

1

SCIENCE OF LOVE, CARE AND NURTURE IN THE EARLY YEARS

AIMS OF THE CHAPTER

1. To explore the practical implications which link to the theoretical concepts of love and nurture in the early years.
2. To understand the science behind brain architecture and links to sensitive and responsive interactions for a child.
3. To explore nurturing attachment and children's emotional, sociocultural and brain development.
4. To link with research on understanding children's emotional development and developing a sense of a child's needs through the lens of nature and nurture.

KEY DEFINITIONS

Listed below are the key definitions that this chapter will cover.

Love	Young children's need for love and care in their early years is usually explained by reference to attachment theory. Love describes a deep sense of affection for our children which means we have their best interests at heart.
Care	For children to achieve their full potential, as is their human right, they need health care and nutrition, protection from harm and a sense of security, opportunities for early learning and responsive caregiving.
Nurture	Nurture refers to the care and attention that children are given while they are growing and developing.
Early attachment	Attachments are the emotional bonds that young children develop with parents and other carers such as their key person.

Emotional development	Emotional development is the emergence of the experience, expression, understanding and regulation of emotions from birth and the growth and change in these capacities throughout childhood.
Brain development (neuroscience)	Brain development is part of the nervous system and refers to the processes that generate, shape and reshape the brain through creating neural pathways, from the earliest stages of embryonic development to adulthood.
Epigenetics	Epigenetics is an emerging science which shows how environmental influences affect the expression of genes, in other words, how a child's experiences modify their inherited genetic DNA makeup.

INTRODUCTION

This chapter explores the concept of both love and nurture in the early years. In the early years of a child's life, we can look to attachment theory (developed by evolutionary theorist John Bowlby) to explain their need for love and care (Bowlby, 1988). It suggests that newborn mammals' survival chances are enhanced by an innate ability to seek care and bond with their primary caregivers. Various neuroscience studies have been conducted to support the importance of early attachments, including Gerhardt (2015) and Music (2017). In works such as Elfer et al. (2003), authors suggest 'key working' or 'primary caregiving', in which each child has a named adult with whom they can form a consistent attachment. According to Ebbeck and Yim (2009), as well as Page (2011), despite some guilt and ambivalence, most parents expect professionals to establish close, responsive relationships with their children when they are absent.

There is a growing thirst from early years professionals to learn about the developing brain and how we nurture children's development, due to wanting to learn much more about children's needs. Nurturing the brain and focusing on child development holistically has recently become a clear way to facilitate early years practice. The main aim of nurturing the early years child is to offer a balance of opportunities for children to help with healthy brain development, maintain a focus on the child's learning capabilities and support every child to reach their full potential throughout life. Research tells us that nurturing an emotional relationship is the primary function needed for intellectual and social growth (Bradbury and Swailes, 2022).

Nurturing the child builds on much of the work around nurturing an emotional relationship, for example, the work of Bowlby (1988), Goswami (2006) and Ainsworth (1978). More recent researchers and academics such as Conkbayir (2017, 2023), Grimmer (2021, 2023) and Zeedyk (2013) are using the science to help us explore child development, the emotional attachment needed and more coherently why it is important to nurture the human brain during the earliest of years. At the most basic of levels, the science and research tells us that relationships which foster an element of warmth, intimacy and happiness form a strong sense of security for the child. Maslow (1970) builds upon this notion and considers the need for physical safety, protection from injury and supplying the basic needs for nutrition, housing and shelter. The evidence from the researchers above shows us that when there is a safe, secure and nurturing environment, children can learn about themselves in a caring and empathetic environment, and this acts as a foundation for their future lives.

NATURE AND NURTURE

Neuroscience, psychology, sociology and education are all contributing to nature/nurture debates in developmental science. There is a conflicting but complementary dialogue between biological factors (nature) and environmental influences (nurture) in human development. Human minds and developmental pathways do not have a fixed cause-and-effect relationship. The environment triggers neurobiological processes, which, in turn, are interpreted differently by each individual. Throughout life, genes and environment interact dynamically. A child's brain will grow most rapidly during the earliest years of their life when nature and nurture work together. Children's brains become more plastic as they develop because of environmental influences and stimulation on physical, emotional, social, cultural and cognitive levels.

Children's brains differ due to their biogenetic uniqueness. Therefore, both nature and nurture are inextricably linked, and both can lead to human growth, development and dysfunction. Children's starting points can be positively shaped by the quality of their environment and how it interacts with them emotionally, socially, physically and cognitively. Despite this, Kagan's (2010) studies indicate that certain brains are more easily triggered than others, making them more vulnerable to experiences. Consequently, attachment and parent/caregiver responses to the child play a critical role in building a solid and positive foundation for the child's future. Children who may have had poor starting points may benefit from early intervention programmes to support the child's best outcomes and promote positive lifelong attachments.

Children benefit from self-critical, reflective and differentiated pedagogies by being observed, noticing and recognising what matters to them, as well as responding positively. When the genes of each child are matched with the environment in which they are developed, an early start is possible. Identifying and addressing hereditary vulnerabilities may even improve their chances of a more positive life path. It was often believed that a child was a blank slate and that their actions could 'mould' their development; every decision, good or bad, shapes a child. As a society, we now acknowledge that children are not blank slates and cannot be moulded in this way. The genetic makeup of an individual influences every aspect of their personality and behaviour. Children's behaviour and development are strongly influenced by their genes from conception onwards. Genes, however, do not completely determine a child's fate – no personality or behaviour is 100% inherited. Children tend to be a certain way due to their genes, such as the amount of sleep they need or the type of personality they have; however, these genetic influences must be able to flourish in an environment that supports them.

EPIGENETICS

Epigenetics and child development are explored at Harvard University's Center on the Developing Child (nd). Researchers are exploring how the environment influences children's experiences that can lead to the expression of their genes. Therefore, genes are no longer considered to be 'set in stone'. Nowadays, as Figure 1.1 shows, both nature and nurture are always intertwined, so the debate between them is no longer relevant. Gene expression is determined by the chemical marks left by the DNA that makes up our genes during child development. In genetics, epigenomes are collections of chemical markers. It is these chemical marks that are rearranged by children's experiences. As a result, genetically identical twins show different behaviours, skills, achievements and health status.

Figure 1.1 The environmental influences on genes and experiences of the child are intertwined

It is important to recognise that epigenetics is a field that explores how early experiences can affect children for the rest of their lives. During child development, epigenetic marks that govern genes and how they express can be rearranged, affecting how those genes release or carry information. Epigenomes can be influenced by positive experiences such as those explored in this book – supportive relationships, love and nurture that create opportunities for learning. Environmental toxins and stressful life circumstances, such as neglect, poverty and severe abuse, can also impact it negatively (Figure 1.2).

THE CHILD'S BRAIN

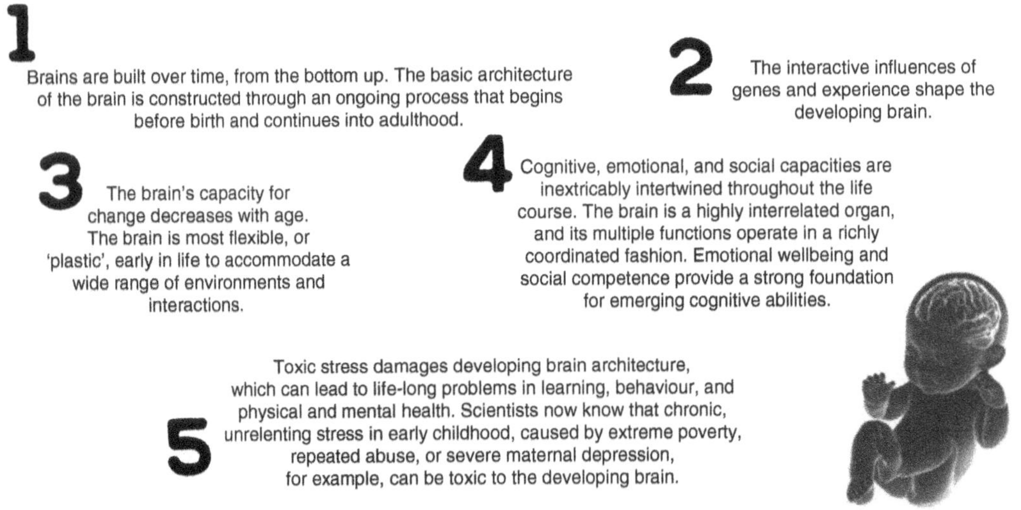

1 Brains are built over time, from the bottom up. The basic architecture of the brain is constructed through an ongoing process that begins before birth and continues into adulthood.

2 The interactive influences of genes and experience shape the developing brain.

3 The brain's capacity for change decreases with age. The brain is most flexible, or 'plastic', early in life to accommodate a wide range of environments and interactions.

4 Cognitive, emotional, and social capacities are inextricably intertwined throughout the life course. The brain is a highly interrelated organ, and its multiple functions operate in a richly coordinated fashion. Emotional wellbeing and social competence provide a strong foundation for emerging cognitive abilities.

5 Toxic stress damages developing brain architecture, which can lead to life-long problems in learning, behaviour, and physical and mental health. Scientists now know that chronic, unrelenting stress in early childhood, caused by extreme poverty, repeated abuse, or severe maternal depression, for example, can be toxic to the developing brain.

Figure 1.2 The science of early brain development can inform investments in early childhood
Source: Adapted by Authors.

The earliest years of a child's life are important for their future health and development. The main reason for this is due to how fast the brain grows, starting before birth and continuing into early childhood. Conkbayir explains that by three years of age, a child's brain is about 80% the size of an adult's and by the age of five, it equates to 90% (2023). Even though the brain continues to develop throughout the life course, the first eight years are critical in being able to build a foundation for learning, health and success.

The development of the brain depends on multiple factors in addition to genes, such as:

- proper nutrition starting from pregnancy;
- exposure to toxins and infections – building immunity;
- the child's experiences with others around them and the immediate impact of the world.

Being responsive and offering nurturing care for a child is the key to supporting health brain development. To be able to nurture a child both in terms of their cognitive and physical development, parents and caregivers need to have access to effective knowledge, support and adequate resources.

There needs to be a continual importance of recognising the experiences from a child's immediate environment for brain development. This means that children are born ready to learn, to develop ongoing skills which are built up over many years. The outcomes of this depends largely on the child's immediate family and their caregivers to help the child develop certain skills to become independent. Brain growth is very much linked to the child's experiences with others within the world. This can be both positive experiences and negative experiences. Therefore, we believe that nurturing care and love are critical for brain growth. Children grow and learn best within a safe and secure environment where they are protected from neglect and from chronic and extreme stress, with plenty of opportunities to be able to play and explore.

Focusing on play, early childhood professionals can work with parents and carers to encourage children in speaking and listening, and playing with and discussing care for their child. Exploring how to nurture a child by making clear links to the child's needs and being able to respond in a sensitive nature helps protect children's brains from stress. Encouraging children to use language, exposing them to books, stories and songs helps them strengthen their language and communication.

However, exposure to stress and trauma can have long-lasting effects for a child's brain, whereas play, environment and loving interactions stimulate brain growth. Ensuring that parents, caregivers and early childhood care providers have the resources and skills to provide safe, stable, nurturing and stimulating care is an important goal. When children are at risk, knowing about child development is key to making sure that they reach key developmental milestones and can ensure that any problems are detected, and early intervention can be sought. It is important to note that even though we have used the term 'developmental milestones', being able to truly nurture a child includes recognition that all children develop at different rates and stages. We want to stress the unique child is of utmost importance and highlight why this is vital.

Birth to 5 Matters: Non-statutory Guidance for the Early Years Foundation Stage, explains that:

Each child is unique, and while we can be guided by an understanding of some general patterns of development from pre-birth into early childhood, progression is uneven and unfolds differently for each individual child. The complex differences for each child mean the pathways toward maturity should be seen more as dancing around a ballroom than climbing a ladder. A child's growth, development and learning are interrelated in complex ways from the moment of conception all the way through infancy to early childhood and beyond. Experiences during the early years strongly influence a child's future development, as development and learning build on what has already been acquired.

(Early Years Coalition, 2021, p. 18)

Harvard University within the Center on the Developing Child explores the concept of why we need to invest in brain development, and nurture child development. The research explores that brains are built over time, beginning before birth, and how playful interactions between adults and children can assist in this development (Center on the Developing Child, 2023). Furthermore, children can learn lifelong skills like resilience, executive functioning and self-regulation through play and loving interactions.

Therefore, there are many ways in which we can nurture our children by giving them early loving and playful experiences. Working alongside parents and carers is an important aspect of being able to give every child the best possible start in life. We can share simple ideas within practice that are developed around love which will, in turn, help the child grow and thrive. For example, babies and young children get a lot out of interactions such as reading, talking, singing and most importantly playing. Being responsive in caregiving, loving and providing a nurturing environment alongside loving touch, such as cuddling, is important, as well as making sure that all children get opportunities for loving touch whenever and wherever they need it. Chapter 4 explores loving touch in more detail. You might like to consider the following case study and reflect upon how you would respond and provide love and nurture.

CASE STUDY

Zara is 4 years old and is a looked after child. When she was 2 years old, it was believed she was at significant risk of harm; however, she now has a stable and happy home, living with her foster parents of nearly 2 years. Zara is just about to join your setting. She finds socialising with other children challenging and is wary of adults.

What might you need to consider when including Zara in your provision?

How might you build a successful relationship with her?

What would be the ingredients for a nurturing environment for Zara?

THE BEGINNINGS OF EMOTIONAL DEVELOPMENT

Emotional development within the early years is entrenched within a child's growing sense of self. Babies and young children initially develop a sense of self-awareness and then self-understanding in the second year of life. By their third year, their emotional collection broadens to encompass self-awareness of emotional traits such as pride, shame, guilt and embarrassment (Lewis, 2000). Early relationships influence how children develop, and close, secure attachments to their carers is important for children's healthy development. According to the *Birth to 5 Matters: Non-Statutory Guidance for the Early Years Foundation Stage*:

Positive relationships support wellbeing and the gradual development of self-regulation. When adults tune in to children's signals and respond sensitively and consistently to meet their needs, children can feel safe, relaxed, and loved. Regular patterns of activities which create routine and help children to know what to expect next also foster a sense of security and self-confidence.

(Early Years Coalition, 2021, p. 19)

It is also important to recognise that children's emotional development is built into the architecture of their brains. Children in our early years settings should be able to see their world as a product of relationships, and these relationships can affect their intellectual, physical, emotional and behavioural development. Professionals develop certain qualities that promote wellbeing and competence of a child, by:

• being focused on individuals;
• making emotional connections to others.

Early secure attachments contribute to the growth of a broad range of outcomes, including a love of learning, a sense of oneself, developing social skills, building successful relationships later in life and developing a sense of empathy and emotional understanding. Sensitive and responsive relationships between child and professional are associated with stronger cognitive skills in young children and in later education the child develops their social competence and work skills. This illustrates the connections being made between social and emotional development. It is important that as professionals we use science to inform our approaches around nurturing positive relationships within an early years environment. We need to include everyone who interacts with children, but also include nurturing each other and recognise that adult relationships and wellbeing are also significant key milestones (Bradbury, 2022). Our own past experiences can also impact our emotional development as the following reflection indicates.

REFLECTIVE PRACTICE EXERCISE

WHY IS TEACHING EMOTIONAL DEVELOPMENT IMPORTANT?

Think about when you were a child. The first time you were asked to stand up in front of children or even share your favourite toy with others. Maybe you noticed someone who needed cheering up or you wanted to go and interact with them. What would have caused you to get emotional and have a meltdown? At the time, you did not want to do these things, and this caused you to get emotional. However, now you do this more willingly. This has been a big step within your own emotional growth, and this growth has been guided by those adults in your life.

Think about those times when you lead your practice to develop strong emotional development and support children in the following ways.

(Continued)

(Continued)

How have these skills influenced practice in your early years setting, supporting the child's home environment and their community and impact on wider society?

Emotional developmental point	Early years setting	Supporting the child's home environment	Community/ Society
Self-awareness			
Social awareness			
Emotional regulation			
Relationship building			
Decision-making			

Now think about those children who may not be given the emotional guidance and how they struggle within those environments. For example, children who have experienced complex trauma often have difficulty identifying, expressing and managing emotions. How might this have impacted their lives and their ability to self-regulate or be resilient? How will your practice change in the light of these reflections?

LOVE, CARE AND NURTURE IN THE EARLY YEARS

Nurturing engages children in the human community in ways that support them to define who they are, what they can become and why they are important to other people (Shonkoff and Phillips, 2000). This can be seen in the words attributed to Bronfenbrenner (cited in National Scientific Council on the Developing Child, 2004a, p. 1):

...in order to develop normally, a child requires progressively more complex joint activity with one or more adults who have an irrational emotional relationship with the child. Somebody's got to be crazy about that kid. That's number one. First, last, and always.

A recent research study by Tamsin Grimmer explores if there is a place for love in early childhood settings (2023). Her research depicted the need for early childhood educators to have a duty of care for the children they educate and look after. The study observed educators who were not afraid to demonstrate their affection for the children by positive touch, which was encouraged by both policy and practice. As discussed in Chapter 4, Chapman and Campbell (2012) recognise physical touch as one of their five love languages. Grimmer's study also highlighted many other factors with regards to love in the early years; however, one aspect highlighted how developing a loving pedagogy empowers children to feel safe, secure, valued listened to and not being seen as powerless but being seen as competent human beings (Clark, 2017; Grimmer, 2023). Much of the work around love in the early years has begun on the shoulders of the pioneering work of Dr Jools Page. As Page (2018, p. 126) asserts,

Professional Love is a complex construction because there are many instances when aspects of love, intimacy and care are overlapping and cannot be compartmentalised, which is why it is difficult to distinguish these – one from another – within actual professional early years practices in any tangible way.

THE CONCEPT OF NURTURING AND LOVE

Nurturing is a concept which is used within the work of theorist Dr Stephen Bavolek (2018). His research, which is embedded in preventative work against child abuse and neglect, can be adapted to our everyday practices. The child is continually learning, and nurturing can enhance their opportunities to learn in a safe and secure environment. For many, nurturing is happening within our settings without us putting that label onto it. However, some settings need to explicitly adopt a nurturing approach. There are many more approaches to child development than just education and looking at it through a holistic lens helps immensely with other aspects of supporting the child. Chapters 2 and 3 explore holistic approaches further.

Different brain systems enhance nurturing by supporting parent–infant attachment, as well as emotional wellbeing, learning and giving attention. It can be easy to think of your primary function as being the child's secondary caregiver, but have you taken the steps to think about the child holistically? Have you reflected on the interactions, the relationships you have built with the child's main caregiver or even involved a discussion around the ethos of nurturing care and what this means to the child, the setting and the main caregiver? Secure attachment can form with any caregiver (parent or professional) who provides security, safety, affection and comfort.

Grimmer (2021, 2023) explores this approach and you can see links between the discussion above and how developing a loving pedagogy within your setting has similar aspects of being able to nurture the child's emotional state. Whilst allowing the child to develop and learn in a safe and positive environment, Grimmer explores this concept looking at children being able to learn. To do this effectively, there are three outcomes to focus on here: children feeling loved in your care, which in turn allows them to become empowered, including feeling confident and being independent, and this leads to them being ready to learn. Ideas of a loving pedagogy resonate with Bronfenbrenner's work (1994); to develop a holistic approach to love and nurture, you need to start with the child. Just like the concept of nurturing, Bronfenbrenner's theory views the child holistically as part of a family and much wider community. He also believed that relationships were at the heart of child development.

WHAT THE SCIENCE TELLS US

The core features of emotional development include the ability to identify and understand one's own feelings, to be able to read and understand one's own emotional states and that of others. This allows a person to be able to manage their own strong behaviours, develop empathy within others and establish and sustain positive relationships (Thompson and Lagattuta, 2006).

A child's emotional development depends on the architecture of their brain, which is shaped by their experiences and the environment in which they live. A fundamental aspect of human functioning is emotion, which is derived from biology and is 'hard-wired' into multiple areas of the nervous system (Gunnar and Davis, 2003). In the earliest years of a child's life, the growing interconnections between brain circuits support the maturation of emotional behaviour. It is during times of feeding, comforting and holding that newborns and young infants experience emotional connections with a caregiver (Shonkoff and Phillips, 2000).

Babies and infants will display distress and cry when they are hungry, cold, wet or, in other ways, uncomfortable. During this age range, babies and infants are incapable of modulating the expressions of their feelings and have limited ability to be able to control their emotions (LeDoux, 2000). The emotional state of babies and young children is much more complex and the 'emotional health of young children is closely tied to the social and emotional characteristics of the environments in which they live' (National Scientific Council on the Developing Child, 2004b, p. 4).

This brings us nicely onto the discussion of love, both in the child's home, but more importantly, within practice, focusing on the role we play as early childhood professionals and how we can love children within the work we do. There is much research which focuses on the interactions we have with children, but Page's research considering whether mothers want professionals to love their children (Page, 2011) allows us to think about the topic and how we position ourselves to provide loving care attachments within our early years settings.

Grimmer explores the languages that we use when we care for children and discusses Chapman and Campbell's (2012) love languages. Even though this is aimed at parents, much of this research can be adopted to our daily practices as Chapter 4 explores. Love and nurture are widely understood within the early years; however, we believe that you need to do both to ensure that children are thriving in their earliest of years. Maslow (1943) identified love and belonging in his hierarchy of needs, which indicates that adopting a loving and nurturing approach can help meet those basic needs.

WHY LOVING, NURTURING RELATIONSHIPS ARE IMPORTANT FOR CHILD DEVELOPMENT

Children's relationships shape the way they see the world and affect all areas of their development. Through relationships with parents, care givers, other family members and other children, they can start to learn about the world that they live in. This is because relationships allow children to express themselves. To cry, laugh and even question, in return, gets something back: a cuddle, a smile and an answer. What children get back allows them to process important information about the world in which they live in, what it is like and learn how to act within this world. This serve and return is vital as they develop further skills on how to communicate, think, learn to understand, behave, show emotions and develop critical social skills. You might like to reflect upon your own interactions and responses by trying the exercise below.

REFLECTIVE PRACTICE EXERCISE

A baby babbling
A child asking questions
A child crying

(Continued)

Responding in a loving, gentle way to these and other situations allows the child to learn about communication, behaviour and emotions.

Think about your daily interactions with children in your setting. How are you showing those foundations of love and nurture with key people and children in your setting?

CHARACTERISING LOVE IN THE EARLY YEARS

Attachment studies have highlighted the significance of Bowlby's Internal Working Model (Bowlby, 1973) and reinforce the importance of love in the early years as providing a template for future relationships. Building attachments position the professional with being able to bond and connect, and attachment becomes a viable concept of early years practice. Within practice, the key person role is key here to providing nurture and love in the early years (DfE, 2024). However, there are multiple definitions of love. In his inaugural speech on love, Professor Michael Gratzke (2015) explains that this is what people say and explores:

'Love is what people say it is', means in a phenomenological sense that people's lived experiences and descriptions of love should be taken seriously by love researchers. Love is what people describe it as being.

(Gratzke, 2015)

Love within an early years setting comes from the ethos of the approaches to nurturing very young children. It could be argued that love needs to form part of the leadership within the setting (Uusiautti and Määttä, 2013). Love in early education serves to create a learning environment where children can be themselves, develop their own resources and reach their potential, and a vital component of a loving early years professional is the ability to see things from the child's perspective (Zombylas, 2007). This links to the interactions between the professional and the child and the wider environment. There is a broader discussion around the influence of positive experiences and perceived happiness of a child, which is widely accepted in the early years and research indicates that positive interventions increase happiness and decrease depression (Seligman et al., 2005). However, nurturing children is so much more than just creating a positive learning environment.

It is important that when we discuss nurture or love we consider whose nurture or love it is. What we are meaning here is a moral dilemma, referring to what constitutes and is perceived to be the common good on raising children. Dewey (1909) suggested that moral education should help children decide what to do and therefore behaviours are transformed into good character. In early education settings, professionals who adopt a loving pedagogy and love-based leadership style also role model love, forgiveness and trust in the relationships they build, which in turn encourages these attributes in children and increases their engagement, productivity and satisfaction (Grimmer, 2021; Prewitt, 2003; Rego et al., 2011). Määttä and Uusiautti (2012) have defined the connection between pedagogical love and authority in the following manner: 'If pedagogical love and pedagogical authority are based on expertise-based respect, the learning atmosphere is warm and encouraging. Mutual respect supports empathy…'. Children relate to the professional because of their expertise and regard the professional as a sort of 'safe mainstay that they can rely on. The [professional] trusts and believes in the [child's] abilities, respects their individuality, and helps them to enhance their balanced development and find their own strengths' (2012, p. 29).

REFLECTION

Love is a fundamental part of a child's emotional, social and cognitive development. The wellbeing of a child is significantly influenced by the presence of a safe and loving environment. A child's development is positively impacted by love in the following ways:

1. **Security in terms of emotions:**
   The foundation for establishing trust and establishing secure attachments is love and affection. A child who feels loved is more likely to develop a strong emotional bond with caregivers, fostering a sense of safety.
2. **Interpersonal and social skills:**
   The experience of love teaches children empathy and compassion. It is easier for them to understand and respond to the emotions of others when they feel loved, which is the basis for healthy interpersonal relationships.
3. **Confidence and self-esteem:**
   Possessing a positive self-image is a result of unconditional love. If a child feels loved, they are more likely to develop confidence, a healthy sense of self-worth and the ability to cope with challenges.
4. **Development of cognitive abilities:**
   Being loved and secure provides a solid foundation for cognitive development. Feeling supported and loved encourages children to explore their environment, ask questions and participate in learning.
5. **Stress regulation:**
   In order to reduce stress, love and emotional support act as buffers. As a result of feeling loved, children are better able to cope with challenges and regulate their emotions, which contributes to their emotional and mental wellbeing.
6. **The development of language:**
   Communication is encouraged in a loving environment. As a result of feeling loved, children are more likely to express themselves verbally, facilitating the development of language and the ability to articulate feelings and thoughts.

(Continued)

7. **Regulation of behaviour:**
   Positive reinforcement contributes to the development of appropriate behaviour. When children feel loved and supported, they are more likely to exhibit positive behaviour.
8. **Developing resilience:**
   Resilience is built through the power of love. When children feel loved, they are more likely to develop effective coping mechanisms that enable them to deal with challenges and setbacks in the future.
9. **The sense of belonging:**
   A sense of belonging is fostered by family and community connections. The development of a strong sense of identity and belonging is more likely to occur in children who feel loved by their families and communities.

A child's development is positively influenced by love in every aspect. As a result, it provides a nurturing environment where children are able to thrive emotionally, socially and intellectually, thereby laying the foundation for a healthy and fulfilling life.

CONCLUSION

Emotional development can affect the whole of child development. Given the small window from conception to five years of age, brain development and the emotional stages linked to this, having caring, responsive relationships, are crucial to nurture from the very beginning. Our role as early childhood professionals is to build on the science and grow loving, nurturing relationships with children.

KEY QUESTIONS

1. To what extent is your practice evidence-based in relation to growing nurturing relationships?
2. How might you ensure your children feel safe and secure in your provision?
3. Would you describe your leadership style as love-based? Why, or why not?

References

Ainsworth, M.D.S. (1978) The Bowlby Ainsworth attachment theory. *Behavioural and Brain Sciences*, 1(3), pp. 436–438.

Bavolek, S. (2018) *Nurturing Skills for Families: Parent Handbook.* Family Development Resources, Inc.

Bowlby, J. (1988) *A Secure Base: Clinical Applications of Attachment Theory.* London: Taylor and Francis.

Bowlby, J. (1973) *Attachment and Loss: Vol. 2. Separation: Anxiety and Anger.* New York, NY: Basic Books.

Bradbury, A. and Swailes, R. (2022) *Early Childhood Theorists Today.* London: Learning Matters.

Bradbury, A. (2022) Nurturing in the Early Years: What the science tells us? *Early Education Journal*, 96(1), pp. 7–9. ISSN 0960-281.

Bronfenbrenner, U. (1994) Ecological models of human development. In Husen, T. and Postlethwaite, T. (Eds.), *International Encyclopedia of Education* (2nd Ed., Vol. 3, 1643–1647). Oxford: Pergamon Press.

Center on the Developing Child (2023) *Brain-Building through Play: Activities for Infants, Toddlers and Children.* Harvard University. https://developingchild.harvard.edu/resources/brainbuildingthroughplay/

Chapman, G. and R. Campbell. (2012) *The 5 Love Languages of Children.* Chicago, IL: Northfield Publishing.

Clark, A. (2017) *Listening to Young Children* (Expanded 3rd edn.). London: National Children's Bureau.

Conkbayir, M. (2017) *Early Childhood and Neuroscience: Theory, Research, and Implications for Practice.* London: Bloomsbury Publishing.

Conkbayir, M. (2023) *The Neuroscience of the Developing Child: Self-Regulation for Wellbeing and a Sustainable Future.* Abingdon: Routledge.

Department for Education (DfE) (2024) *Statutory Framework for the Early Years Foundation Stage.* Available at: https://www.gov.uk/government/publications/early-years-foundation-stage-framework--2

Dewey, J. (1909) *Moral Principles in Education.* Cambridge, MA: The Riverside Press.

Early Years Coalition (2021) *Birth to Five Matters Non-statutory Guidance to the Early Years Foundation Stage.* Available at: https://birthto5matters.org.uk/wp-content/uploads/2021/03/Birthto5Matters-download.pdf (accessed on 1 February 2023).

Ebbeck, M. and Yim, H. (2009) Rethinking attachment: Fostering positive relationships between infants, Toddlers and their primary caregivers. *Early Child Development and Care*, 179, 889–909.

Elfer, P., Goldschmied, E. and Selleck, D. (2003) *Key Persons in the Nursery: Building Relationships for Quality Provision.* London: David Fulton.

Gerhardt, S. (2015) *Why Love Matters: How Affection Shapes a Baby's Brain* (2nd edn.). Hove: Routledge.

Goswami, U. (2006) Neuroscience and education: From research to practice? *Journal of Nature Review Neuroscience*, 7(5), pp. 406–411.

Gratzke, M. (2015) Love is what people say it is. Gratzke Inaugural Speech. April 27. Love Research Hull. Available at: https://archive.org/details/MichaelGratzkeInauguralHull2015 (Accessed on 1 October 2017).

Grimmer, T. (2021) *Developing a Loving Pedagogy in the Early Years: How Love Fits with Professional Practice.* Abingdon: Routledge.

Grimmer, T. (2023) Is there a place for love in an early childhood setting? *Early Years*, 42(5).

Gunnar, M.R. and Davis, E.P. (2003) Stress and emotion in early childhood. In Lerner, R.M., Easterbrooks, M.A. and Mistry, J. (Eds.), *Handbook of Psychology: Developmental Psychology* (Vol. 6, pp. 113–134). John Wiley & Sons, Inc. https://doi.org/10.1002/0471264385.wei0605

Kagan, J. (2010) Once more into the breach. *Emotion Review*, 2(2), pp. 91–99.

LeDoux, J. (2000) Emotion circuits in the brain. *Annual Review of Neuroscience*, 23, pp. 155–184.

Lewis, M. (2000) Self-conscious emotions: Embarrassment, pride, shame and guilt. In Lewis, M. & Haviland–Jones, J.M. (Eds.), *Handbook of Emotions* (2nd ed., pp. 623–636). New York, NY: The Guilford Press.

Määttä, K. and Uusiautti, S. (2012). Pedagogical authority and pedagogical love – Connected or incompatible? *International Journal of Whole Schooling*, 8(1), pp. 21–33.

Maslow, A. (1970) *Motivation and Personality* (2nd edn.). New York, NY: Harper & Row.

Maslow, A. (1943) A theory of human motivation. *Psychological Review*, 50(4), pp. 370–396.

Music, G. (2017) *Nurturing Natures: Attachment and Children's Emotional, Sociocultural and Brain Development.* Abingdon: Routledge.

National Scientific Council on the Developing Child (2004a) *Young Children Develop in an Environment of Relationships.* Working Paper No. 1. Available at: https://developingchild.harvard.edu/wp-content/uploads/2004/04/Young-Children-Develop-in-an-Environment-of-Relationships.pdf

National Scientific Council on the Developing Child (2004b) *Children's Emotional Development Is Built into the Architecture of Their Brains.* Working Paper No. 2. Available at: https://developingchild.harvard.edu/wp-content/uploads/2004/04/Childrens-Emotional-Development-Is-Built-into-the-Architecture-of-Their-Brains.pdf

Page, J. (2011) Do mothers want professional carers to love their babies? *Journal of Early Childhood Research*, 9(3), pp. 310–323.

Page, J. (2018) Love, care and intimacy in early childhood education and care. *International Journal of Early Years Education*, 26 (2), pp. 123–124.

Prewitt, V. (2003) Leadership development for learning organizations. *The Leadership & Organization Development Journal*, 24(2), pp. 58–61.

Rego, A., Ribeiro, N., Pina, M. and Jesuino, J.C. (2011) How happiness mediates the organizational virtuousness and affective commitment relationship. *Journal of Business Research*, 64(5), pp. 524–532.

Seligman, M.E.P., Steen, T.A., Park, N. and Peterson, C. (2005). Positive psychology progress. Empirical validation of interventions. *American Psychologist*, 60(5), 410–421.

Shonkoff, J.P. and Phillips, D.A. (Eds) (2000) *From Neurons to Neighborhoods: The Science of Early Childhood Development.* Washington, DC: National Academy Press.

Thompson, R.A. and Lagattuta, K.H. (2006). Feeling and understanding: Early emotional development. In McCartney, K. and Phillips, D. (Eds.), *Blackwell Handbook of Early Childhood Development* (pp. 317–337). Malden, MA: Blackwell Publishing.

Uusiautti, S. and Määttä, K. (2013) Love-based leadership in early childhood education. *Journal of Education, Culture and Society*, 1, pp. 109–120.

Zeedyk, S. (2013) *Sabre Tooth Tigers and Teddy Bears: The Connected Baby Guide to Understanding Attachment.* Dundee: Suzanne Zeedyk Ltd.

Zombylas, N. (2007) Emotional ecology: The intersection of emotional knowledge and pedagogical content knowledge in teaching. *Teaching and Teacher Education*, 23, pp. 355–367.

2

WHAT CONSTITUTES LOVE AND NURTURE IN THE EARLY YEARS?

AIMS OF THE CHAPTER

1. To recognise loving and nurturing practices and to better understand the interconnection of love and nurture.
2. To understand the vital importance of relationships and to be aware of the impact of attachment needs and trauma.
3. To acknowledge the role love and nurture play in promoting mental health and wellbeing.
4. To understand the benefits to children of a loving and nurturing approach.

KEY DEFINITIONS

Listed below are the key definitions that this chapter will cover.

Attachment-aware	When adults understand the neuroscience of attachment and adopt relational practices that are loving and nurturing.
Adverse Childhood Experiences (ACEs)	Traumatic experiences that occur during childhood and have a negative impact on the child.
Loving pedagogy	A child-centred approach underpinning all aspects of our provision which holds children in mind and enables them to feel loved.
Mental health	This term encompasses our psychological, social and emotional wellbeing.
Pedagogy	Our approach, everything we do in practice from the ethos we foster to the teaching methods we employ.

Social, emotional and mental health (SEMH)	The term 'SEMH' is used to describe a range of different needs relating to children's mental health and wellbeing. Children with SEMH may have difficulty with emotional regulation, forming attachments or building relationships or have an underlying mental health issue.
Trauma	Trauma describes going through an event or experience that is stressful, frightening or distressing.
Trauma-responsive practice	When policy and practice is informed by and responds to an understanding of the impact on trauma.
Wellbeing	When we refer to wellbeing, we are talking about how positively someone feels about life, themselves and how comfortable or healthy they are.

INTRODUCTION

We use the term 'pedagogy' to describe our approach and what underpins our teaching choices. When we use the term in relation to a loving pedagogy, we describe it as 'the practice of educators' combining the 'caring aspects of our role' with our everyday practices (Grimmer, 2021, p. 3). Although it describes an ethos, a loving and nurturing pedagogy can also be seen in practical ways because real love involves loving actions. For example, we foster a sense of belonging through displaying photos of our children and their families in our settings, we build warm loving relationships and use positive touch within our interactions, and we hold our children in mind, planning activities or exciting provocations which we know they will enjoy (Grimmer, 2021).

This chapter explores love and nurture in terms of our practice. It will link with our pedagogy, build on the discussion around attachment that began in Chapter 1 and acknowledge the fact that love and nurture are inseparable. It will remind readers that relationships are vital and loving and nurturing approaches are attachment-aware and trauma-responsive. This chapter will also consider the role that love and nurture play in promoting children's mental health and wellbeing and share the many benefits of a loving and nurturing approach.

LOVING AND NURTURING AS HOLISTIC PRACTICES

For many people, loving and nurturing interactions form the foundation of their practice and are at the heart of their ethos, yet they are not always thought about or discussed. Sadly, some professionals ignore the emotional world of the child as they focus more on academic achievement or learning specific things. Clearly there is room for both; however, we need to view children holistically to fully support them within early childhood. Loving and nurturing children is about the whole child – their physical, emotional, cognitive, social and spiritual development – and we cannot consider one part of a child in isolation.

Adopting a holistic ethos where love and nurture underpins everything in an overt way is the best option. When we do this, it will infiltrate all aspects of our provision from our policies and procedures to the way we greet children and families and the sense of belonging they feel in our setting. Chapter 3 explores nurture through a holistic lens in more detail.

Our children have all grown up in different families with unique lived experiences and reflecting upon the whole child as part of a family and community is another way we can love and nurture them holistically. Bronfenbrenner's ecological systems model (see Figure 2.1) reminds us of the huge impact external influences can have on children (1979). If we can better understand how influences, such as relationships, stress, poverty, neglect and the emotional environment can affect children, we can plan more effectively for them and use appropriate strategies to support and intervening early if needed.

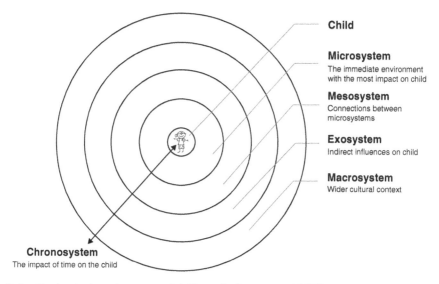

Figure 2.1 Ecological systems model (Bronfenbrenner, 1979)

REFLECTIVE PRACTICE EXERCISE

Draw upon Bronfenbrenner's model (see Figure 2.1) to reflect upon a child in your care.

Draw five concentric circles and write their name in the centre of the circle.

1. Consider their microsystem – what are or who has the most direct influence on them? This will probably include their close family members and perhaps your setting.
2. Next consider their mesosystem – how are these microsystems connected to each other? For example, how do you as a setting interact with the child's parents and carers?

(Continued)

(Continued)

3. Now consider their exosystem – what external influences are there on them beyond their immediate situation, for example, wider family, community, media or religious groups they belong to.
4. Next consider the macrosystem – this is the wider cultural context that they have been born into, for example, has the pandemic or the cost of living crisis impacted their family?
5. Now think about the chronosystem – this is the impact that time may have had on the child, for example, a child growing in the 2020–2030 decade will be impacted by technology and artificial intelligence, whereas this had very little impact on a child growing up in the 1980s.
6. Lastly, reflect upon this whole process. What insights have you gained about the child and family? How can you use this information to better support the child in your provision?

THE INTERCONNECTEDNESS OF LOVE AND NURTURE

When we consider ideas of love and nurture within an early childhood context, they appear to be inseparable from each other. Where does loving stop and nurturing begin, and vice versa? Often the phrase *lovingly nurtured* is used when thinking about tending to a garden which implies a longer-term commitment. To lovingly nurture our children, we meet their immediate needs with a long-term view, just as we might nurture a seed, knowing that we are helping a plant or flower to grow. Our focus is broadly on the bigger picture; however, we still need to manage the detail as we feed and water the seedling and make sure the environment offers enough light and nutrients daily for it to grow.

This is about intentional practices, from the way we choose to interact with children to enjoying children's company and spending time together. The preschool case study below demonstrates how they used information from the child's home and family to inform their music choices throughout the day and how this was an intentional way of enabling children to feel at home.

PRESCHOOL CASE STUDY

As part of our settling in process we ask for lots of information from families, including information about the child's routine, their likes and dislikes, how the child prefers to be held or calmed or if they have any specific toy, song or comforter to help them sleep. We also invite the family to share a photo to display and ask if the family listen to any specific music at home. We then add this music to the playlist for that child's room. Several times we have

(Continued)

witnessed a child stop what they were doing and smile or even spontane-ously start dancing or go and stand beside their family photo when they hear a certain song played, as it reminds them of home. These simple things can help to foster a sense of belonging.

Early childhood professionals also need to think about how they interact with children. Our tone of voice and the amount of warmth in our voice are more important than the actual words we choose to use, because they often speak the truth about our feelings. There is a game you can play with children, where you say something in a tone of voice and with facial expressions that imply the opposite – for example, saying in an encouraging and warm tone with a smile on your face, 'Mmmm, this cake is disgusting!' This is a particularly useful game to play with autistic children who might find reading people's emotions difficult. So, practising this through play is helpful and is a loving way to nurture our children's emotional literacy.

Another intentional practice is to view the behaviours of children as communicating their needs and ensuring we base our responses on this view. For example, if, while working as a childminder, we heard the baby crying, we would want to work out why and try a few things to see if it helped. We might first try picking them up and talking in soft soothing tones in case they wanted company. Then we may try gently rocking them, patting their back or stroking their cheek in case they were tired. Perhaps we would adjust our position whilst holding them in case they were feeling uncomfortable, or prepare a bottle in case they were hungry. The more attuned we become to the baby, the more we are able to interpret their cries and ascertain what they are communicating. Thus, through these nurturing practices, we demonstrate our love for children. Chapter 6 explores the idea of behaviour as communication in more detail as it considers how a relational approach nurtures our children and enables them to develop within loving relationships.

LOVE AND NURTURE ARE GROUNDED IN RELATIONSHIPS

A wealth of neuroscientific evidence and educational theory backs up the importance of attachments in early childhood (Bowlby, 1953; Gerhardt, 2015; Music, 2017; Zeedyk, 2020); however, in simple terms, this is about relationships. As Read reminds us, 'We now know due to advances and research on brain development that the key building blocks for emotional wellbeing, good mental health and future success in life are developed through close, loving and intimate relationships' (2014, p. 3). Keeping relationships with children at the forefront of our practice helps us to build secure attachments and love and nurture them.

Prioritising relationships sounds easy to do; however, sometimes our daily activities get in the way. For example, how many times have you said to a child when they ask you to play or do something for them, 'In a minute… I'm just finishing this…' or 'Not now…' It reminds me of the classic children's book, *Not Now, Bernard*, by David McKee (1980), which is actually more of a message to parents and carers than a storybook for children! It tells the story of Bernard who has found a monster in his back garden, but his parents are too busy to notice. They keep saying, 'Not now Bernard...' then Bernard gets eaten by the monster and they still don't notice... they even put the monster to bed!

Building relationships is a two-way process and necessitates the adult being 'available to the child, emotionally and physically, attentive to their needs and attuned to them' (Grimmer, 2021, p. 123). An example of this 'attentive love' as Noddings would describe it (2002) is when an educator notices a child looks uncomfortable and questions, 'Do we need to change your nappy now?' or remembers a child has just visited their Nana and asks, 'Did you have a lovely time with Nana?' This is drawing upon your knowledge of a child and engaging in respectful interactions with them, responding sensitively to their needs, context, wants and emotions.

REFLECTIVE PRACTICE EXERCISE

Invite someone to video you during a short interaction with a child. Then watch it back and reflect upon these questions:

How did you attune to the child?
Did you hold the child in mind during the interaction?
Were you engaged in attentive love?
What did it look like?
In what ways was the interaction respectful and responding sensitively to the child?
What might you keep doing or do differently in the future?

Holding others in mind in this way is a natural aspect of being in relationship with another person. We do this with our friends and family when we think about other people, even when we are not with them; for example, when out shopping, we see a gift and think so-and-so would love that, or we check in with our sibling after we know they had a hospital appointment, or we pop round with some flowers if we notice our friend is feeling down. In an early childhood context, holding children in mind outlines our loving and nurturing approach and reminds us of our role, responding to children in the moment, being present for them and attending to their needs (Grimmer, 2021). Grimmer's research noted ways that children were held in mind in a practical sense, '...adults would notice if a child was absent or arrived late; adults would compliment a child's jumper or ask them about their older sibling or new baby at home' (2023, p. 9). These simple 'noticings' made an enormous difference on a daily basis and contributed to children's feelings of wellbeing and belonging. They felt loved, special and empowered.

Effective communication is a foundation of this and engaging in serve-and-return conversations at various different moments during the day will not only role model how to communicate but will also build our relationship as we get to know children better. What this would look like in a setting is an adult spending time with children, getting down to their level and engaging in small talk or chatting with them, sometimes commenting or providing a running commentary for what they are doing and engaged in, but often just enjoying their company, sharing jokes, smiles and taking it in turns to communicate. If we are working with very young children, we can still role model conversations and engage in so-called proto-conversations which are turn-taking episodes before a child can talk (Bateson, 1975; Tronick et al., 1980; Yoo et al., 2018). These serve-and-return conversations show the child that it's my turn to talk, now it's your turn to talk... my turn... your turn... and so on. We might be using sounds, words and/or gestures and signs to communicate and the conversation doesn't necessarily need to make sense, but it is teaching children the essential skills needed for the future.

When early childhood professionals adopt a relational approach such as a loving pedagogy, they are actually helping their children to learn through love (Grimmer, 2021; Henderson and Smith, 2022). This builds on the view that we are social beings and actively seek out social interactions from birth. Actually, this is true from before birth – Italian research, from the University of Turin and the University of Parma, demonstrated that twins interact with each other in the womb from around 14 weeks gestation (Weaver, 2011). By the time we are born, we recognise our mother's voice (Hepper et al., 1993) and very young children prefer to look at faces over other stimuli (Frank et al., 2009). As Trevarthen (2008, p. 16) explains, 'Infants are ready at birth to take turns in a "dialogue" of movements with a loving parent. They are attracted to extended engagement with human gestures, and sympathetic to many emotions— resonating to the impulses and qualities of movement; imitating, seeking to play an active part in proto-conversations or playful duets of agency'. So, we are not only born into a social world, but we are active social agents within it. Thus, our social relationships are a vital component of child development.

ATTACHMENT NEEDS AND TRAUMA

Attachment theory highlights the central importance of relationships and the impact our early relationships have on the rest of our lives (Bowlby, 1953) and understanding about attachment can help us to comprehend why children act or react the way they do, and help us to remain more sensitive and attuned to their needs. In addition to having different attachment styles (Ainsworth and Bell, 1970), there is now a wealth of research into the impact of adversity and the importance of building early relationships and attachments (Felitti et al., 1998; Hertzman, 2013; Schilling et al., 2008). Many of our children will have experienced Adverse Childhood Experiences (ACEs), which are defined as, 'highly stressful events or situations that occur during childhood and/or adolescence' (Brennan et al., 2019, p. 4). The term 'ACEs' was coined by the American Adverse Childhood Experiences Study which found a relationship between these experiences at a young age and multiple health risks later in life, including links to the leading causes of death in adults (Felitti et al., 1998). ACEs can include one-off experiences such as parental separation, more ongoing situations like having an ill or incapacitated parent or threatening and traumatic experiences, for example, witnessing domestic violence, or being the victim of abuse, bullying or facing discrimination. It is generally accepted that many potentially traumatic experiences could have a significant effect on children's wellbeing, for example, experiencing a bereavement at a young age, poverty, being in care and experiencing racism (Nicholson et al., 2023).

Therefore, sadly, there are many different situations that babies, children or young people are exposed to that can lead to childhood adversity or trauma and this is more common than one might imagine. According to Bellis et al. (2014), half the UK population have experienced at least one ACE, with 9% having experienced four or more. This equates to approximately three children in a typical class of 30 students. This is the negative side of the story; the good news is that secure attachment has a positive impact on academic achievement and success in future life. As Bergin and Bergin note, secure attachments are '…associated with greater emotional regulation, social competence, and willingness to take on challenges, and with lower levels of ADHD and delinquency, each of which in turn is associated with higher achievement' (2009, p. 141). Schools and settings need to not only be aware of the negative impact attachment needs and trauma can have but also recognise the many benefits to adopting a relational approach such as a loving pedagogy.

REFLECTIVE PRACTICE EXERCISE

To what extent have you and your team received training on ACEs and the impact of trauma?

Reflect upon your key children. Do you know much about their backgrounds and lived experiences?

When talking about families with the children, do you take into account that this could trigger unwanted feelings or past trauma?

Would you describe your approach as trauma-responsive? Why or why not?

BECOMING MORE ATTACHMENT- AND TRAUMA-RESPONSIVE

Many authors highlight the importance of adopting a more attachment-aware and trauma-informed approach within education, citing a wealth of research which confirms the positive impact this would have on children (Bergin and Bergin, 2009; Grimmer, 2022; Grimmer and Geens, 2022; Jarvis, 2020; Kelly et al., 2020; Little and Maunder, 2021; Zsolnai and Szabób, 2021). Sadly, at the time of writing, educational policy in England has not yet been hugely influenced by such research; however, Scotland's educational system is leading the way, encouraging a whole-school and setting focus on nurturing and/or trauma-informed approaches. They introduce their summary of resources to support schools in this approach stating,

Nurturing and trauma-informed approaches can have a positive impact on attainment and social and emotional competences and confidence. At the heart of nurture and being trauma-informed is a focus on wellbeing and relationships and a drive to support the growth and development of children and young people, many of whom come from areas of disadvantage and require additional targeted support to close the equity gap.

(Education Scotland, 2023)

Despite a lack of national policy, many local authorities, boroughs, Multi-Academy Trusts, schools, settings and other educational organisations are drawing upon research and information relating to trauma and attachment with a commitment to make local practice better informed and inclusive. In Derbyshire, their Attachment Aware Schools (AAS) programme began in 2014 and relates to an approach grounded in attachment theory, which prioritises relationships and is informed by an understanding of both child development and neuroscience (Kelly et al., 2020). It aims for schools to adopt an approach whereby adults build secure attachments with pupils, seek to understand their needs and respond using practices such as emotion coaching (Figure 2.2). 'AAS schools report that this has led to "happier children" who feel more valued and listened to within more nurturing and caring environments' (Kelly et al., 2020, p. 351).

Regardless of whether policymakers promote these practices, we can become more aware of the impact of trauma and amend what we do in the light of them. Nicholson et al. (2023) suggest that although being trauma-informed is important, we need to move beyond simply being informed by this information and actually act on it. Being trauma-responsive is better because this speaks of action and actually changing our practices in the light of trauma and past experiences (Nicholson et al., 2023).

Figure 2.2   Creating a safe haven and secure base
Source: Created by Tamsin Grimmer.

One of the best ways to begin is to educate ourselves and learn more about how ACEs, attachment and trauma might impact our children. We can ensure our own ethos and approach is responsive and nurturing children through adopting a loving pedagogy does this. Children and families need to feel welcomed and that they belong in our provision and we can prioritise relationships, getting to know our children and families really well. Children need to know we are trustworthy and dependable, so demonstrate this by being consistent in boundary setting, present for the children and available to them. We can also establish an emotionally enabling environment where children feel accepted, free to be themselves and their emotions are validated.

By being responsive to trauma and informed by our understanding of the neuroscience of attachment and trauma, we can ensure our settings and schools become a secure base for our children. As Figure 2.3 demonstrates, there are simple changes we can make to our provision which help us to be trauma-responsive.

In addition, how securely attached a child feels will have a direct influence on their behaviour and ability to self-regulate. Being aware of this can help us to adapt our expectations accordingly and we can use a range of strategies to intervene sensitively. This is explored more fully in Chapter 6.

Trauma-responsive practice

- Foster relationships
- Recognise behaviour as communicating needs
- Provide a predictable routine
- Encourage participation and give children a voice
- Aware of backgrounds and potential triggers when talking about families
- Avoid assumptions about past
- Incorporate regular movement and sensory activities
- Provide a calm environment
- Play together

Figure 2.3 Trauma-responsive practice
Source: Created by Tamsin Grimmer.

LINKS WITH MENTAL HEALTH AND WELLBEING

Loving relationships form the basis for emotional wellbeing and good mental health (Read, 2014), therefore, when we nurture children as part of a loving pedagogy, we promote their positive mental health and wellbeing. Everyone has mental health, just as everyone has physical heath; however, the term 'mental health' is often only used in conjunction with diagnosable conditions and is therefore sometimes viewed in a negative way. As Hogg and Moody remind us,

> Being mentally healthy is a positive state that enables us to enjoy life and deal with challenges' and 'Being mentally healthy in infancy and early childhood enables babies and young children to understand and manage emotions, to experience nurturing, meaningful relationships, and to explore, play and learn. (2023, p. 3)

Defining mental health in this way offers a clear link with wellbeing. Sometimes wellbeing is thought of in terms of life satisfaction or happiness; however, as The Children's Society warns '…though it is easy to slip into a shorthand of happiness, well-being is about so much more than this' (2015, p. 3). For example, when experiencing bereavement, an adult may rate themselves with low wellbeing, whereas they could be working through the normal stages of grief (Kubler-Ross, 1969) which would hugely influence this rating. On a different day, that same person may rate themselves more positively. Measuring mental health and wellbeing in terms of feelings could be viewed as too simplistic because there are many factors involved, not simply how an individual may feel at any given time.

Public Health England (2015, p. 6) describe mental wellbeing as,

more than the absence of mental illness and is inextricably linked with an individual's emotional, physical and social wellbeing. It is influenced by their resilience and physical health, relationships and the wider social, economic, cultural and environmental conditions in which they live.

This holistic definition is helpful and links with Hogg and Moody's ideas around being mentally healthy in early childhood, 'Paying attention to, and being curious about a baby or young child's mental health can help us to identify concerns about their relationships, wider health, development, and safety and to act to address these issues quickly' (2023, p. 8). Early identification of needs makes an enormous difference to children and families.

Therefore, we need to take children's wellbeing seriously within early childhood and measure it, regularly, over time. This is because we value what we measure. As the Children's Society (2015, p. 11) highlight, 'If schools [and settings] do not measure the wellbeing of their children, but do measure their intellectual development, the latter will always take precedence'. If we are only measuring things like counting skills or whether or not a child can recognise their name, we are not valuing the most important things. Many early childhood professionals use tools like the *Leuven Scales of Wellbeing and Involvement* (Laevers, 2005) or the *Sustained Shared Thinking and Emotional Wellbeing* rating scale (Siraj et al., 2015), and measuring wellbeing is part of how they provide a supportive emotional environment to their children and families.

It should be noted that some difficulty arises when measuring wellbeing and mental health in the early years. In children under three, it is often measured in terms of temperament, when parents identify any problem behaviours with the assumption that wellbeing is the absence of such behaviours (Department of Health, 2014). However, considering wellbeing in the context of problems, or even the absence of problems, is a deficit approach and does not reflect the holistic nature of wellbeing. If parents are identifying their child's temperament and behaviours, it depends on their interpretation and recognising any issues and may also be an indication on the parent's own state of mind. Having said this, it could be argued that for a very young child to be and remain mentally healthy, they need a caregiver who co-regulates their emotions and provides a loving and nurturing environment, which a parent may find difficult if their own mental health and wellbeing is low.

The UK charity Mind suggests that 1 in 4 people will experience a mental health problem of some kind each year in England (2023) and statistics from the Mental Health Foundation (2023) state that 50% of lifetime mental illness starts by age 14. Statistics such as these remind us of the prevalence of mental health problems and highlight the importance of helping children to be mentally healthy in early childhood to enable them to develop strategies which stand them in good stead for their future life (Hogg and Moody, 2023). The Mental Health Foundation (2023) identify several ways that society can put preventative measures in place to help reduce the prevalence of mental health difficulties and three of them are very relevant for us within early childhood:

1. Helping parents nurture their children
2. Protecting children from trauma
3. Educating children to understand and manage their emotions.

In their report *Prevention and Mental Health*, they state, 'There may be key opportunities to prevent [mental health problems] from happening by introducing protective factors – for instance, equipping parents to nurture their children in a non-judgemental way, ensuring a reliable adult presence at school, or providing professional and peer support early' (Mental Health Foundation, 2023, p. 8). Therefore, when we nurture children through adopting a loving pedagogy, become a co-regulator, teach children strategies to develop self-regulation and work with families in a loving and nurturing way, we are doing all we can to promote good mental health and wellbeing for our children.

THE BENEFITS OF NURTURE WITHIN A LOVING PEDAGOGY

It feels strange writing this section, because surely the benefits of nurture within a loving approach would be obvious to all; however, it is important to emphasise the implications of what we do and how we do it and the impact this has on our children. In adopting this approach, children will feel loved, which White identifies as vital as he states, the 'Fundamental need, desire, hunger, longing and potential gift of every human is to love and be loved' (2008, p. 45). It could be argued that children have a right to be loved because through loving and being loved, children have the opportunity to trust in themselves and in others and may respond more positively to any demands placed upon them by their loved one (Liao, 2006).

Children need to be loved unconditionally. Regardless of their behaviour. Regardless of their feelings towards us. Unconditional love says I love you because you are you and nothing you can say or do will stop me from loving you. Children should never feel they have to earn our love, behave a certain way or be a different person in order for us to love them. Unconditional love is a choice we make and involves more than just a depth of emotions, it is demonstrated through our nurturing practices. This is highlighted in the extracts below from research (Grimmer, 2023).

PRESCHOOL CASE STUDY – HOW FEELING LOVED IMPACTS TRANSITIONS INTO THE SETTING

When researching if there was a place for love in an early childhood setting, I (Tamsin) undertook some intimate conversations, a little like interviews, with early childhood professionals. Here are a couple of extracts from this research:

We are very friendly and welcoming and we try to engage all the children and get down to their level and I just think it makes them feel at ease and then, you know they can thrive and enjoy their experience when they're here and I think we do build up really good rapport with them and, you know, they all arrive so happily and separate so happily I think you can see that there is that sort of connection and whether it's, you know, they feel loved... I think we do act in a loving way

(Continued)

towards them, you know we're like a little community really and they all feel a part of that which is important so I guess in that sense they feel, yeah, they feel very much loved in the setting.

(Grimmer, 2023, p. 9)

Building those secure bonds and relationships for us is beneficial for the children, I think they feel secure and it means that they can arrive in the morning and they can know that everybody here they trust and they know and they're kind of keen to come in and get involved, I think if they feel trust, if they feel loved and cared for by the team, it makes coming into the setting easy.

(Grimmer, 2023, p. 10)

Loving involves more than just feelings and emotions; it is generally accepted that to love someone also involves actions (Vincent, 2016) and this is where nurturing others really comes into play. It could be argued that nurture is the practical application of love; when we want the very best for someone, hold them in mind and try to speak their love languages (Grimmer, 2021). We try to instil in our children a sense of belonging, which is essential for positive mental health and wellbeing (Shifron, 2010), and we build children's self-esteem and help them to feel special, which is beneficial in all aspects of our lives (Orth and Robins, 2022).

Acting in loving ways and role modelling nurturing practices also teaches children loving, kind and caring pro-social behaviours. This is important because they are attitudes and dispositions we want to foster and grow for the sake of future society! As I (Tamsin) share in my book *Developing a Loving Pedagogy*,

I strongly believe that children should grow up in a society where they are loved and this needs to continue within their early childhood settings and schools. If educators love the children in their care and understand how they prefer to be loved, they will better understand how to relate to them and will do so more appropriately, which, in turn, will enable the children to learn more effectively.

(Grimmer, 2021, p. 2)

As we nurture children on a daily basis, they learn they will be listened to, which offers them a sense of agency and enables them to feel empowered. In doing so, we are also putting Article 12 of the United Nations Convention on the Rights of the Child into practice, which is summarised as, 'Every child has the right to express their views, feelings and wishes in all matters affecting them, and to have their views considered and taken seriously' (UNICEF, 1989). We want children to not only have a voice but to be active agents and know that using their voice may result in action (Mashford-Scott and Church, 2011) (Figure 2.4).

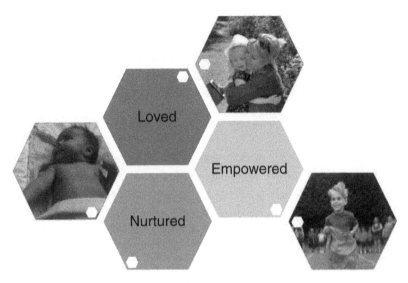

Figure 2.4 Loved, empowered, nurtured
Source: Created by Tamsin Grimmer.

Another benefit of nurturing children within a loving pedagogy is that working in this way embraces a very natural way of engaging with children. Many early childhood professionals would say they love the children they work with and want the best for them, so in the words of Page (2013, p. 192) it gives us, 'Permission to love them'.

There are many ways of practically nurturing and loving children:

- Building secure attachments and relationships
- Spending time together and being attuned to them
- Prioritising our children and focusing on them
- Paying attention to their likes and dislikes
- Listening to our children and, whenever possible, acting on what they say
- Being compassionate
- Empathising and validating their emotions.

CONCLUSION

This chapter has explored how loving and nurturing practices are interconnected and it would be impossible to remove nurture from a loving approach. It has argued that relationships are at the heart of what we do as early childhood professionals and developing an awareness of the impact of attachment needs and trauma will not only inform our practices but also transform them and enable us to be responsive to children's needs. Loving and nurturing practices also contribute to promoting positive mental health and wellbeing, in addition to the many other benefits listed. A really important message here is that we can, and do, make an enormous difference to the lives of our children. By building secure attachments and lovingly nurturing our children, we are contributing to their future success, not just within school but also within life.

KEY QUESTIONS

1. In what ways do we lovingly nurture our children?
2. Does each child feel listened to and valued as part of our setting?
3. Do we respect individuality and our families' unique funds of knowledge? How do we demonstrate this?

References

Ainsworth, M.D. and Bell, S.M. (1970) Attachment, exploration, and separation: Illustrated by the behavior of one-year-olds in a strange situation. *Child Development*, 41(1), pp. 49–67.

Bateson, M.C. (1975) Mother-infant exchanges: The epigenesis of conversational interaction. *Annals of the New York Academy of Sciences*, 263, pp. 101–113.

Bellis, M., Lowey, H., Leckenby, N., Hughes, K. and Harrison, D. (2014) Adverse childhood experiences: Retrospective study to determine their impact on adult health behaviours and health outcomes in a UK population. *Journal of Public Health*, 36(1), pp. 81–91.

Bergin C. and Bergin, D. (2009) Attachment in the classroom. *Educational Psychology Review*, 21, pp. 141–170.

Bowlby, J. (1953) *Childcare and the Growth of Love*. London: Penguin Books.

Brennan, R., Bush, M. and Trickey, D. (2019) *Adversity and Trauma-Informed Practice: A Short Guide for Professionals Working on the Frontline*. Young Minds.

Bronfenbrenner, U. (1979) *The Ecology of Human Development: Experiments by Nature and Design*. Boston, MA: Harvard University Press.

Department of Health (2014) *Starting Well – Pregnancy to 5 Years*. Available at: https://www.gov.uk/government/uploads/system/uploads/attachment_data/file/277569/Starting_Well.pdf

Education Scotland (2023) *Nurture and Trauma-Informed Approaches: A Summary of Supports and Resources*. Available at: https://education.gov.scot/improvement/learning-resources/nurture-and-trauma-informed-approaches-a-summary-of-supports-and-resources/

Felitti, V., Anda, R., Nordenberg, D., Williamson, D., Spitz, A., Edwards, V., Koss, M. and Marks, J. (1998) Relationship of childhood abuse and household dysfunction to many of the leading causes of death in adults: The Adverse Childhood Experiences (ACE) Study. *American Journal of Preventive Medicine*, 14(4), pp. 245–258.

Frank, M.C., Vul, E. and Johnson, S.P. (2009) Development of infants' attention to faces during the first year. *Cognition*, 110(2), pp. 160–170.

Gerhardt, S. (2015) *Why Love Matters: How Affection Shapes a Baby's Brain* (2nd edn.). Hove: Routledge.

Grimmer, T. (2021) *Developing a Loving Pedagogy in the Early Years: How Love Fits with Professional Practice*. New York, NY: Routledge.

Grimmer, T. (2022) *Supporting Behaviour and Emotions in the Early Years: Strategies and Ideas for Early Years Educators*. Abingdon: Routledge.

Grimmer, T. (2023) Is there a place for love in an early childhood setting? *Early Years*. https://doi.org/10.1080/09575146.2023.2182739

Grimmer, T. and Geens, W. (2022) *Nurturing Self-regulation in Early Childhood: Adopting an Ethos and Approach*. Abingdon: Routledge.

Henderson, N. and Smith, H. (2022) *Relationship-Based Pedagogy in Primary Schools: Learning with Love* Abingdon: Routledge.

Hepper, P.G., Scott, D. and Shahidullah, S. (1993) Newborn and fetal response to maternal voice. *Journal of Reproductive and Infant Psychology*, 11(3), pp. 147–153.

Hertzman, C. (2013) The significance of early childhood adversity. *Paediatrics & Child Health*, 18(3), pp. 127–128.

Hogg, S. and Moody, J. (2023) *Understanding and Supporting Mental Health in Infancy and Early Childhood – A Toolkit to Support Local Action in the UK*. UNICEF,.

Jarvis, P. (2020) Attachment theory, cortisol and care for the under-threes in the twenty-first century: Constructing evidence-informed policy, *Early Years*, 42(4–5), pp. 450–465.

Kelly, P., Watt, L. and Giddens, S. (2020) An attachment aware schools programme: A safe space, a nurturing learning community. *Pastoral Care in Education*, 38(4), pp. 335–354.

Kübler-Ross, E. (1969) *On Death and Dying*. New York, NY, The Macmillan Company.

Laevers, F. (2005) *Well-Being and Involvement in Care Settings: A Process-Oriented Self-Evaluation Instrument*. Leuven: Kind & Gezin and Research Centre for Experiential Education.

Liao, M. (2006) The right of children to be loved. *The Journal of Political Philosophy*, 14(4), pp. 420–440.

Little, S. and Maunder, R. (2021) Why we should train teachers on the impact of childhood trauma on classroom behaviour. *Educational and Child Psychology*, 38(1), pp. 54–61.

Mashford-Scott, A. and Church, A. (2011) Promoting children's agency in early childhood education. *Novitas-ROYAL*, 5(1), pp. 15–38.

McKee, D. (1980) *Not Now Bernard*. London: Andersen Press.

Mental Health Foundation (2023) *Children and Young People Statistics*. Available at: https://www.mentalhealth.org.uk/explore-mental-health/statistics/children-young-people-statistics

Mind (2023) *Mental Health Facts and Statistics*. Available at: https://www.mind.org.uk/information-support/types-of-mental-health-problems/statistics-and-facts-about-mental-health/how-common-are-mental-health-problems/

Music, G. (2017) *Nurturing Natures: Attachment and Children's Emotional, Sociocultural and Brain Development*. Abingdon: Routledge.

Nicholson, J., Perez, L., Kurtz, J., Bryant, S. and Giles, D. (2023) *Trauma-informed Practices for Early Childhood Educators: Relationship-Based Approaches that Reduce Stress, Build Resilience and Support Healing in Young Children*. New York, NY: Routledge.

Noddings, N. (2002) *Starting at Home: Caring and Social Policy*. London: University of California Press.

Orth, U. and Robins, R.W. (2022) Is high self-esteem beneficial? Revisiting a classic question. *American Psychologist*, 77(1), pp. 5–17.

Page, J. (2013) Permission to love them. In Page, J., Clare, A. and Nutbrown, C. (Eds.), *Working with Babies and Young Children from Birth to Three*. London: SAGE.

Public Health England (2015) *Measuring Mental Wellbeing in Children and Young People.* Available at: https://assets.publishing.service.gov.uk/government/uploads/system/uploads/attachment_data/file/768983/Measuring_mental_wellbeing_in_children_and_young_people.pdf

Read, V. (2014) *Developing Attachment in Early Years Settings: Nurturing Secure Relationships from Birth to Five Years* (2nd edn.). Abingdon: Routledge.

Schilling, E., Aseltine, R. and Gore, S. (2008) The impact of cumulative childhood adversity on young adult mental health: Measures, models, and interpretations. *Social Science and Medicine,* 66(5), pp. 1140–1151.

Shifron, R. (2010) Adler's need to belong as the key for mental health. *Journal of Individual Psychology,* 66(1), pp. 10–29.

Siraj I., Kingston D. and Melhuish E. (2015) *Assessing Quality in Early Childhood Education and Care – Sustained Shared Thinking and Emotional Well-Being (SSTEW) Scale for 2–5-Year-Olds Provision.* London: Trentham Books.

The Children's Society (2015) *The Good Childhood Report.* Available at: https://www.york.ac.uk/inst/spru/research/pdf/GCReport2015.pdf

Trevarthen, C. (2008) The musical art of infant conversation: Narrating in the time of sympathetic experience, without rational interpretation, before words. *Musicae Scientiae,* (Special issue), pp. 15–46.

Tronick, E., Als, H. and Brazelton, T.B. (1980) Monadic phases: A structural descriptive analysis of infant–mother face to face interaction. *Merrill-Palmer Quarterly,* 26(1), pp. 3–24.

UNICEF (1989) *United Nations Convention on the Rights of the Child.* Available: http://www.unicef.org.uk/Documents/Publication-pdfs/UNCRC_PRESS200910web.pdf

Vincent, J. (2016) Perspectives on love as a component of professional practice. *Scottish Journal of Residential Child Care,* 15(3), pp. 6–21.

Weaver, J. (2011) Social before birth. *Scientific American Mind,* 21(6), p. 13.

White, K. (2008) *The Growth of Love.* Abingdon: The Bible Reading Fellowship.

Yoo H., Bowman Dale. A. and Oller D. K. (2018) The origin of protoconversation: An examination of caregiver responses to cry and speech-like vocalizations. *Frontiers in Psychology,* 9, p. 1510.

Zeedyk, S. (2020) *Sabre Tooth Tigers and Teddy Bears: The Connected Baby Guide to Understanding Attachment.* Dundee: Suzanne Zeedyk Ltd.

Zsolnai, A. and Szabób, L. (2021) Attachment aware schools and teachers. *Pastoral Care in Education,* 39(4), pp. 312–328.

3

THE NURTURED CHILD

AIMS OF THE CHAPTER

1. To recognise how we build a healthy and strong emotional relationship with children.
2. To develop children through a nurturing lens, including how they treat themselves, others and their environment.
3. To look at nurturing as a critical endorsement for early years practice and understanding why nurturing is so important.
4. To understand how nurturing the child links to child development by building on the child's emotional relationships for intellectual and social growth.

KEY DEFINITIONS

Listed below are the key definitions that this chapter will cover.

Nurturing children	Nurturing means more than giving your child food, shelter and clothing. It is about building a healthy and strong emotional relationship (attachment) between you and your child and promoting holistic development.
Children's basic needs	Children must feel safe, with their basic survival needs being met: shelter, food, clothing, sleep, medical care and protection from harm.
Child development	Child development involves the biological, psychological and emotional changes that occur in human beings between birth and adolescence.
Holistic child development	Holistic child development views the child as a whole and covers all aspects of development including their social, emotional, physical, mental and intellectual growth.
Social development	Social development in early childhood is about building relationships and developing social competence. It is an important part of a person's overall health, wellbeing and happiness throughout their life.

Emotional development	Emotional development represents a specific domain of child development. It is a gradual, integrative process through which children acquire the capacity to understand, experience, express and manage emotions, and to develop meaningful relationships with others.
Children's wellbeing	Children's wellbeing is a combination of their physical, mental, emotional and social health and views the child holistically.
Empathy	Empathy is the capacity to understand or feel what another person is experiencing from within their frame of reference, that is, the capacity to place oneself in another's position.
The voice of the child	The child's voice is a phrase used to describe the real involvement of children and young people. It means more than seeking their views, which could just imply the child saying what they want; instead, it is about acting upon their views.
The rights of the child	The UN Convention on the rights of the child (UNICEF, 1989) upholds children's rights all over the world. The four core principles of the Convention are non-discrimination; devotion to the best interests of the child; the right to life, survival and development; and respect for the views of the child.
Play	Play underpins learning and all aspects of children's development. Through play, children develop in all areas including their emotions and creativity, language skills and social and intellectual skills.

INTRODUCTION

This chapter explores the concept of nurturing from the perspective of the child. Children's lives can be transformed by nurturing. It improves the lives of some of the United Kingdom's most vulnerable children, as well as helping those with mild to moderate social, emotional and mental health needs. Children develop a sense of self-worth and connect with others through nurture. By enabling children to learn, play and communicate in a safe context, nurture is enabling them to thrive.

To develop social and emotional skills that will enable children to do well at school and engage successfully with peers, nurture provides a range of opportunities and enables them to deal with life's trials and tribulations with greater confidence. In some settings, it may take the form of a set of activities geared towards specific groups of children; in others, it may take the form of a whole approach which focuses on wellbeing. Attachment theory and neuroscience inform the concept of nurture. This chapter underlines the significance of social environments in influencing social and emotional skills, wellbeing and behaviour. Empathy, structure and fairness are all attributes of a nurturing ethos within a setting.

MEETING CHILDREN'S BASIC NEEDS

A child's physical and emotional development depends on several basic needs being met (Maslow, 1943). Children's health and development are very important during their earliest years. Healthy development means that children of all abilities, including those with health needs and disabilities, can grow where their social, emotional and learning needs are being met. To be able to meet a child's needs, it is important to provide a safe and loving home and spend time playing, singing, reading and communicating. Additionally, a child's developmental needs can be met by proper nutrition, outdoor play areas and adequate sleeping and resting places.

To continuously meet the needs of their children, professionals must work alongside parents and carers to develop effective parenting practices. In addition, it is essential that we as professionals consider that parents choose to parent their children in a cultural and individual way, and how we work with them to achieve the outcomes of nurturing the children. The provision of care that children need to grow and develop well and to be happy and healthy, however, works well across diverse families and in diverse settings. According to a comprehensive report *Parenting Matters* (Breiner et al., 2016) that examined the evidence in scientific publications, the following key components have been identified to help parents and carers support their child's healthy development:

- Responding to the needs of children
- The ability to show warmth and sensitivity
- Routines and expectations in the household
- The importance of sharing books with children, communicating with them and having a language rich culture
- Assuring health and safety
- Discipline should be applied appropriately without being harsh.

Children's wellbeing and healthy development are fundamentally dependent upon a parent–child relationship as well as the family environment, including the primary caregivers. The caregivers of children provide them with protection and care from birth. When a child's brain is rapidly developing, parents and caregivers have a greater impact on their life than at any other time. During this period, children are immersed in a context of significant ongoing developments.

Your early childhood setting must get to know the children and families in order to nurture them fully. Children in your care benefit from the knowledge parents and carers bring. The engagement of parents has long been at the forefront of early childhood policy and practice, according to Thompson and Simmons (2023). However, they go on to explain that there is an impression that parents are a homogeneous group and that if they follow the processes set out by the early years setting, their children will settle and succeed (McWayne et al., 2022, cited in Thompson and Simmons, 2023). It is crucial that early years professionals have good relationships with parents and carers, according to Cattan et al. (2022). Our relationships with parents, carers, families and the wider professionals working with the child must be strengthened for the child to be a nurtured child.

In the current political climate, support for children and families in the early years is more crucial than ever before. We are nurturing children who are emerging from a world pandemic and entering a cost-of-living crisis. Health, social care and education are all impacted by the nurturing care you provide every day. In the following case study, Caroline outlines how Bright Horizons have adopted a Nurture Approach to try and address these issues.

CASE STUDY

Caroline Wright, Director of Early Childhood at Bright Horizons, provides a detailed account of how they fostered a Nurture Approach within Bright Horizons UK.

The Nurture Approach: Empowering adults to support children's holistic wellbeing and development.

Brief Description: Nurture Approach is a professional development programme, developed by Bright Horizons UK in partnership with a clinical psychologist.

The programme focuses on child development, neuroscience and helping adults to understand the impact of their role in supporting children's emotional wellbeing through building strong, supporting relationships (Figure 3.1).

WHERE DID WE START AND WHY?

Our approach constantly evolves, as we strive to create an environment where everyone can flourish. It has become apparent as we emerge from the post-COVID world, that the needs of the children and the wellbeing of the workforce have to be prioritised.

We recognise that we need to adapt and flex our thinking to reflect research, policy and changes in society, to ensure we're always considering our colleagues' and our children's needs. We developed the Nurture Approach programme, focusing on children's social and emotional needs, through four distinct ages and stages, whilst recognising that all children are unique. Current thinking suggests that we must lay a secure foundation for children's emotional wellbeing and development, and the Nurture Approach helps practitioners to understand how to provide this secure foundation through their day-to-day practice in our settings.

The programme covers children's key developmental needs and shows practitioners how to identify healthy emotional development and indicators of wellbeing. We consider what our role is in meeting a child's needs, when everything is going well and when they are experiencing change, loss or significant life events. We teach practitioners how to recognise early signs of difficulty or disruptions in a child's development.

The programme is informed by Stuart Shanker's (2016) work on self-regulation, which suggests that when an individual's stress levels are too high, various systems for thinking and metabolic recovery are compromised. The signs of dysregulation show up in the behaviour, mood, attention and physical wellbeing. 'Nurture' from our pedagogical perspective is about validating emotions rather than distracting from them.

(Continued)

We developed the programme because we know that it is important to 'meet children where they are' in the moment. The Nurture Approach helps practitioners to consider where the child's 'emotional needs' are in our newly developed 'emotional triangle of needs', so that we can meet them where they are developmentally.

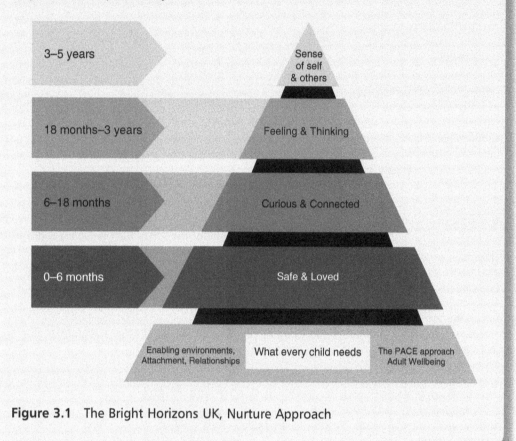

Figure 3.1   The Bright Horizons UK, Nurture Approach

NURTURE THROUGH A HOLISTIC LENS

Providing nurturing care to a child is one of the most important opportunities we can provide as an early childhood professional. According to the concept of nurture, it is important to consider the child's social environment. As a result, their social and emotional skills, wellbeing and behaviour are significantly affected. In early childhood development, concrete foundations are laid as children learn new things every day. It is almost impossible for early childhood professionals not to think about the end goal, but the time that is based in the now makes the greatest impact on the child.

We must ensure that children are allowed to succeed and reach their full potential, which means giving full attention to all aspects of their development. The ability to default back to a child's intellectual abilities may exist during the earliest years, but it is also important for a child to acquire skills such as:

- emotional intelligence;
- confidence;
- social competence;
- compassion;
- fine and gross motor coordination;
- creativity;

and many other skills. . ..

Every child is unique, and it is important to recognise this. There are several characteristics that define a child's uniqueness in the world, such as their personality traits or exceptional talents. The alignment of a child's interests, skills and uniqueness, with areas to develop, is therefore critical to guiding them through the opportunities we provide within our settings that focus on their personal development.

It is important to reflect the holistic development of the child when considering love and nurture. This includes a child's cognitive, linguistic, social, emotional and physical growth for their overall development. By nurturing the brain and supporting healthy brain development, a child can be prepared to handle any challenge or requirement they may encounter on a day-to-day basis, which makes the case to recognise the importance of holistic development in the early years child rather than later in life. Right after a child is born, a newborn brain and the structures within the brain are quite similar to that of an adult brain (Gilmore et al., 2018). As Knudsen explains,

> Experience exerts a profound influence on the brain and, therefore, on behavior. When the effect of experience on the brain is particularly strong during a limited period in development, this period is referred to as a sensitive period.

> (Knudsen, 2004, p. 1412)

Therefore, when a child starts their developmental years, especially the 'sensitive periods', their experiences contribute to the wiring of the brain which supports future abilities and skillsets.

Holistic development aims to nurture and expand a child's full potential with the abilities that will help them lead a successful and positive life. The reason why this is so important is to establish a social adaptability alongside the emotional intelligence to help them surpass their fears of being able to work as a team with other children.

Here are some other reasons why holistic development is important as a child grows:

- Instils confidence to counter pressure of daily challenges.
- Creates a bundle of prolific neural connections which promote physical, social, intellectual and emotional development.
- Builds social and emotional competence and physical growth and helps attain cognitive enlightenment.
- Promotes emotional and psychological wellbeing and instils compassion.
- Lays the foundation for academic successes taking on board children's own abilities and steps in life.

INTENTIONALLY NURTURING CHILDREN

Nurturing children begins before birth and continues throughout life. However, nurturing practices may not come naturally to everyone. The Nurturing Care for Early Childhood Development Framework (2018) launched by the World Health Organization, UNICEF and the World Bank Group promotes five interrelated and essential components: health, nutrition, safety, early learning and giving responsive care. Nurturing Care aims to support the developmental needs of children in the first formative years of a child's life.

The Nurturing Care framework outlines ways in which we can nurture children. In addition, the following are three intentional ways in which adults can learn to nurture a child:

1. Empathy – This is the capacity to understand or feel what another person is experiencing from within their frame of reference, that is, the capacity to place oneself in another's position. We need to observe the actions of others, recognise how they might be feeling, then demonstrate that we understand those feelings. The following quotation attributed to the psychologist Alfred Adler is often shared – Empathy involves 'seeing with the eyes of another, listening with the ears of another, and feeling with the heart of another'. Empathy develops over time and it is difficult for young children to empathise, when they do not yet have a full understanding of their own and others' feelings. We can help them to develop this by observing their feelings, naming and validating those feelings and role modelling being empathetic. For example, saying, *'I wonder if you are angry because Hamza broke your toy...'* or *'I would feel frustrated if my tower kept falling down too...' Empathy is explored further in the next section.*

2. Positive touch – Human touch is a necessity for all of us. Positive touch can include hugs, gentle tickles, high fives and gentle touches on back, arms, etc. As Chapter 4 explores, touch contributes to the development of a child's self-esteem and brain development. Positive touch tells a child they are important, valued and noticed.

3. Routine – This provides consistency and structure in children's lives. Well-established routines for mealtimes, playtimes and bedtimes helps to nurture children because they understand the expectations placed upon them and will feel more in control of their environment. Through repetition and the predictability of routine, children feel secure and anticipate what is to come next. Having a regular routine also helps to reduce anxiety in children.

LINKING TO THE EARLY YEARS FOUNDATION STAGE

There is a statutory framework in England that must be followed called *The Early Years Foundation Stage Statutory Framework* (DfE, 2024). Additionally, there are a few non-statutory guidelines that provide additional guidance regarding how to adhere to and approach the statutory guidelines. *Birth to 5 Matters: Non-Statutory Guidance for the Early Years Foundation Stage* (Early Years Coalition, 2021) is one of these guidance documents. We have chosen this one to guide you through how the holistic child is placed at the centre of the curriculum and nurtured in the context of their learning.

Using such guidance allows you to reflect upon how you are putting the child at the centre of your practices and allowing nurture to flourish before any formal discussions about learning have taken place. As a rule, children will develop and learn in a manner that is typical for their age and stage of development. Nevertheless, learning does not progress in a straight, pre-dictable and linear manner. A child may go backwards in one area of development while making significant progress in another. Balanced development cannot be expected across all areas, and the balance is likely to shift from one area to another.

Nurturing all children in your care requires giving them a voice and promoting their inclusion. According to *Birth to 5 Matters* (Early Years Coalition, 2021, p. 9), 'Inclusion is a process of identifying, understanding and breaking down barriers to participation and belonging'. As part of inclusive practice, there are many aspects of nurturing a child that are involved, such as anticipating, paying attention, responding to and reflecting upon the needs and interests of all children. Another aspect of providing a nurturing holistic approach is to provide a suitable environment within which children can play.

NURTURING THROUGH PLAY

Children have the right to play. A child's right to play is enshrined in Article 31 of the United Nations Convention on the Rights of the Child (UNCRC) (UNICEF, 1989).

Play helps children's development. Play is a natural and enjoyable way for children to keep active, stay well and be happy. Play that is freely chosen helps children and young people's health and development. To be able to have good physical and mental health and to learn life skills, they need various unstructured play opportunities from birth (Play England, 2020). This can also be seen by one of early childhood's pioneers Friedrich Froebel who states:

I wanted to educate people to be free, to think, to action for themselves.

(Froebel in Lilley, 1967, p. 41)

According to Froebel, the child has the freedom to determine their own actions based on the laws and demands of the play they are involved in. In this way, the child is able to feel independent and autonomous (Froebel in Liebschner, 1992). As Froebel saw it, free play helps children think for themselves, make choices, solve problems and pursue their own interests and talents. Froebel's thoughts on free play are consistent with the work of Grimmer (2021), who explores that children must feel love within their learning environment in order to feel secure and free to play and learn. In the diagram below (Figure 3.2), the child explores their environment by being confident and empowered within their learning environment.

Feeling Loved   Empowered   Ready to Learn

Figure 3.2 Developed by Aaron Bradbury: Depiction of a child feeling loved within their early years setting, becoming empowered and ready to learn and play
Source: Grimmer (2022a).

In freely chosen play, a child decides and controls their own play according to their own instincts, imagination and interests. Adults are not required to manage their play. In the eyes of a child, there is no right or wrong way to play. Children benefit from free play in terms of their health, wellbeing and development. We need to take into account many aspects of understanding the world from the child's perspective in order to nurture a child's development. This is where Froebel stresses the importance of play as a central part of human development.

> Play is the highest level of child development. It is the spontaneous expression of thought and feeling. It constitutes the source if all that can be benefit the child... At this age play is never trivial; it is serious and deeply significant.

> (Froebel in Lilley, 1967, p. 84)

The importance of play for young children is well known to early years professionals. Problem solving, social learning and delightful discovery experiences can all be found in play. Play allows children to practise skills with familiar objects as they hone their skills through repetition and familiarity. For example, during a play episode involving playdough, in addition to developing fine motor skills using tools and rolling actions, the children also strengthen their language skills through the conversation about making a pretend meal or playing with the playdough. Additionally, it is a time of exploration during which children explore new ways of using objects or thinking about concepts.

Children's growth and development can be supported during the day by adults observing and interacting with them while they play. And playing together can be fun. Early childhood professionals are aware that being close to children and sharing their enjoyment can help build trust. Children's language and critical thinking skills are developed through natural conversations, during which they are able to ask questions and share their thoughts.

Since there are so many possibilities, you might feel tempted to participate in children's play as soon as it begins – you may, however, risk disengaging children if you do this. Julie Fisher talks about the importance of interacting and not *interfering* in our children's play (2016). Therefore, it is important to consider how you participate in a child's activity.

REFLECTIVE PRACTICE EXERCISE

Pause while children are playing.

Reflect upon what they are doing, saying, possibly thinking or what they might be trying to achieve.

Think about how you could engage in this play? What would the implications be for the children? Are there any benefits for them? Or any risks?

What is the best way forward?

As a facilitator, you should participate in play respectfully and add value to a child's experience. By maintaining consistency in your approach, children will be able to anticipate what is to come. Furthermore, it is essential that children have the opportunity to think and speak for themselves. By actively listening to them, you will be able to learn about their interests, skills and strengths. This information can be used to develop more responsive environments and activities to meet the unique needs of each child.

CHILDREN'S RIGHTS

As part of the UNCRC, children's rights are recognised as well as the right for them to grow up in the spirit of peace, dignity, tolerance, freedom, equality and solidarity (UNICEF, 1989).

There are 54 articles in the Convention. In these articles, you will find provisions pertaining to the rights of children in all aspects of their lives, including civil, political, economic, social and cultural rights. Additionally, it discusses the need for adults and governments to work together to ensure that all children have access to all their rights. Furthermore, the UNCRC has been ratified by the greatest number of countries in the world. All UN member states except for the United States of America have ratified the Convention.

Every child in the United Kingdom has been entitled to over 40 specific rights since 16 December 1991, when the treaty entered into force in the United Kingdom. The rights included in the Convention apply to all children and young people, with no exceptions.

The following are included:

- the right to life, survival and development;
- the right to have their views respected, and to have their best interests considered at all times;
- the right to a name and nationality, freedom of expression and access to information concerning them;
- the right to live in a family environment or alternative care, and to have contact with both parents wherever possible;
- health and welfare rights, including rights for disabled children, the right to health and health care and social security;
- the right to education, leisure, culture and the arts;
- special protection for refugee children, children in the juvenile justice system, children deprived of their liberty and children suffering economic, sexual or other forms of exploitation.

(Play Scotland, 2023)

CHILDREN DEVELOPING EMPATHY

To develop empathy, one must cultivate and nurture the ability to understand and share the feelings of others (Bradbury, 2022). As a result, it is crucial for the formation of strong relationships, the facilitation of effective communication and the promotion of an inclusive and harmonious society. Individuals who are empathetic can connect on a deeper level, providing support and validation to those in need. There is growing evidence that nurturing emotional relationships are essential for both intellectual and social development. In addition to the well-established work of Bowlby (1979) and Ainsworth (1978), other researchers and academics have contributed to this field (some of which we examine in greater depth elsewhere in this book). Furthermore, individuals such as Conkbayir (2017), Goswami (2006) and Zeedyk (2013) are using neuroscience to help us understand how the human brain develops during its infancy. In its most basic form, scientific research indicates that relationships which foster warmth, intimacy and happiness are beneficial to the development of a child's sense of security. Moreover, this is in line with the work of Maslow (1970), who had emphasised the importance of physical safety, protection from harm, as well as providing food and shelter for basic needs. The mounting evidence indicates that children learn empathy and care when they are raised in an environment that is safe, secure, empathetic and nurturing. In the end, this leads to the development of a reflective child who can link their own wishes, communicate their own thoughts and feelings and develop relationships of their own.

> People who are empathetic are more attuned to the subtle social signals that indicate what others need or want.

> (Goleman, 1996, p. 43)

It has been demonstrated in Dr Bavolek's research (cited in Bradbury and Swailes, 2022) that empathy is the foundation for supporting child and parent relationships. A child's empathy helps them cooperate with others around them, allows them to build friendships and helps them learn how to make moral decisions. It may also be argued that this is an important component of lifelong development and that the ability to develop social and emotional skills is equally beneficial to adults. Let us now examine how children develop empathy.

Empathy begins with self-awareness. By understanding our own emotions and experiences, we will be able to relate to others who may be experiencing similar circumstances. Being present in the moment and practising mindfulness can also enhance empathy by enabling us to listen and understand others without judgement. Another important aspect of empathy development is active listening. During this process, you must fully concentrate on the speaker, acknowledge their feelings and respond with compassion and understanding. As we actively listen, we create a safe space in which individuals can express themselves and feel heard, thereby strengthening the bond between them.

According to Bradbury (2022), empathy is important for connecting with others, as well as helping them, but it may have evolved in conjunction with a social antenna. What we are witnessing here is a child looking for social aspects of other children, thereby becoming the antenna. Empathy develops naturally in children, but it must also be nurtured in order for them to be able to understand and feel it. From birth, babies reflect the emotional states and expressions of those around them. In the words of Zeedyk (2012), 'babies are born connected'. As babies begin to reflect the emotional states and expressions of others, the mirror neuron system develops and strengthens. As young as 18 hours old, infants are often responsive to other infants in distress. Early childhood professionals who work in a baby room will recognise this; when one baby cries, the other babies in the room also cry. Our mirror neurons are firing up and the foundations of empathy are developing (Grimmer, 2022b).

To cultivate empathy, we must also step outside our own perspectives and attempt to see the world from others' perspectives. It is possible to achieve this goal by exposing oneself to diverse experiences, cultures and viewpoints. It is helpful to broaden our understanding and empathy towards others by participating in activities that encourage empathy, such as volunteering, participating in community projects or learning about different social issues. In order to develop empathy, it is essential to practise it in everyday interactions. It is important to recognise that small acts of kindness, such as offering a helping hand, expressing gratitude or expressing appreciation, have a significant impact on someone's wellbeing. Empathy requires us to be aware of our own biases and to actively challenge them to cultivate a more inclusive and empathic outlook.

REFLECTIVE PRACTICE EXERCISE

Look at this picture of a baby below:

The baby is looking and focusing on something. It could be an adult who has their attention or even an object which they are focusing on. Perhaps they are looking at someone whom they love. Whatever the child is looking at, imagine how the world looks from their perspective. Imagine what it is like to be so small. Imagine how they feel. If this baby were in your setting, what might gain their attention? Which adults would they be drawn to? How might they feel in your setting? Why?

Empathise with the child and consider what is important from the child's perspective, then reflect upon these elements in your own setting.

Children can develop empathy through activities that encourage them to appreciate and understand different perspectives in educational settings (see Figure 3.3). It is crucial to teach empathy at an early age to develop a generation of empathetic and compassionate individuals who can navigate complex relationships and contribute positively to society. Ultimately, empathy development requires self-reflection, active listening, exposure to diverse perspectives and practice in everyday interactions. The cultivation of empathy can lead to a world that is more compassionate and understanding, where individuals feel valued, supported and connected to one another. Science has now demonstrated that humans are born with a hard-wired 'map' that relates to their genetics, environment and prenatal experiences. Essentially, babies learn to recognise and respond to emotional cues when they are exposed to a safe, supportive environment, with nurturing, supportive adults, from before they are born. When babies and young children exchange gestures (such as a smile), they begin to realise that they are different from us and can perform different (or similar) tasks as we do. A sense of self is formed as a result of this process. Empathy is based on the understanding that we can all experience different emotions and feelings (Bradbury, 2022).

BIRTH TO AGE 2

Read them stories, describe and label their feelings, physical positive touch, hugs and cuddles.

3– 4 YEAR OLDS

Continue to read stories, talk about emotions, use visuals, physical positive touch, teach feeling words, hugs and cuddles.

5 – 7 YEAR OLDS

Use visuals and pictures, continue to read stories, embrace diversity, understand how children observe others, teach feelings words, physical positive touch, hugs and cuddles.

Figure 3.3   Key strategies on how to teach empathy to children

SEEING THE WORLD THROUGH A CHILD'S EYES

We can create an environment of peace, love and calmness by learning to view the world from the perspective of a child. We were challenged by Maria Montessori to 'follow the child' (1942). We must be able to understand how the children in our care think, feel and react to be able to do this.

REFLECTIVE PRACTICE EXERCISE

Here is an exercise we invite you to try:

Take a picture or video of the setting from the height of your children using your smartphone. In the case of a very young child, this can be very dramatic. When you look around the environment, you will notice how different the furniture looks, how the displays appear from below. It will probably look like a scene from *Jack and the Beanstalk* and feel as if giants are living here. In the early years of a child's life, they may feel overwhelmed, powerless and left without a voice.

As the above reflection demonstrates, the world appears different through the eyes of a child. Not only are adults taller and stronger than young children, but they are also the ones who provide them with the necessities of life daily. There is a constant cycle of saying yes and no; one minute you are paying attention to one child and the next minute you are distracted by another. It is common for us adults to have difficulty understanding what our children are saying, and they will always find ways in which to get our attention and communicate by making choices based on their own experiences.

Children learn to recognise the needs of others as well as their own, to communicate with words and to develop skills that foster independence when they are young. It is common for them to cry, smile or coo at first because they do not yet have words. Besides words, most young children communicate their needs with adults through tears, heart-warming smiles, tantrums, pouting and other means. It is at this point that they begin to realise that they have a unique voice. Efforts are being made to foster respectful communication, independence and self-reliance.

CONCLUSION

Love and nurture should always be about empowering young children. As part of our role as early years professionals, it is important to continually think about many aspects which are crucial for children's development including stimulation, parent–child interactions, child-directed and focused applications, early learning and supporting positive parenting (Engle et al., 2011). Linking a collective approach to nurturing care with parents and carers strengthens opportunities for nurturing and enhances child development. Examples of this include the Nurturing Care for Early Childhood Development Framework developed by the World Health Organization, UNICEF and the World Bank Group (2018), which promotes early learning and responsive caregiving.

KEY QUESTIONS

1. In what ways do we lovingly nurture our children?
2. Does each child feel listened to and valued as part of our setting?
3. Do we respect individuality and our families' unique funds of knowledge? How do we demonstrate this?

References

Ainsworth, M. (1978) The Bowlby-Ainsworth attachment theory. *Behavioural and Brain Sciences*, 1(3), pp. 436–438.

Bowlby, J. (1979) The Bowlby-Ainsworth attachment theory. *Behavioural and Brain Sciences*, 2(4), pp. 637–638.

Bradbury, A. (2022) *Nurturing in the Early Years: What the Science Tells Us*. Early Education. Number 69.

Bradbury, A. and Swailes, R. (2022) *Early Childhood Theories Today*. London. Learning Matters.

Breiner, H., Ford, M. and Gadsden, V. (Eds.) (2016) *Parenting Matters: Supporting Parents of Children Ages 0–8*. National Academies of Sciences, Engineering, and Medicine; Division of Behavioral and Social Sciences and Education; Board on Children, Youth, and Families.

Cattan, S., Fitzsimons, E., Goodman, A., Phimister, A., Ploubidis, G. and Wertz, J. (2022) *Early Childhood Inequalities* (Vol. 1). Institute for Fiscal Studies.

Conkbayir, M. (2017) *Early Childhood and Neuroscience Theory. Research and Implications for Practice.* London: Bloomsbury.

Department for Education (DfE) (2024) *Statutory Framework for the Early Years Foundation Stage.* Available at: https://www.gov.uk/government/publications/early-years-foundation-stage-framework--2

Early Years Coalition (2021) *Birth to Five Matters Non Statutory Guidance for the Early Years Foundation Stage.* Available at: https://birthto5matters.org.uk

Engle, P., Fernald, L., Alderman, H., Behrman, J., O'Gara, C., Yousafzai, A., Cabral de Mello, M., Hidrobo, M., Ulkuer, N., Ertem, I. and Iltus, S. (2011) Strategies for reducing inequalities and improving developmental outcomes for young children in low-income and middle-income countries. *The Lancet,* 378 (9799), pp. 1339–1353.

Fisher, J. (2016) *Interacting or Interfering? Improving Interactions in the Early Years.* Maidenhead: Open University Press.

Gilmore, J., Knickmeyer, R. and Gao W. (2018) Imaging structural and functional brain development in early childhood. *Nature Reviews Neuroscience,* 19(3), pp. 123–137.

Goleman, D. (1996) *Emotional Intelligence: Why It Can Matter More than IQ.* London. Bloomsbury.

Goswami, U. (2006) Neuroscience and education: From research to practice. *Journal of Nature Review Neuroscience,* 7(5), pp. 406–411.

Grimmer, T. (2022a) Chapter 2, Urie Bronfenbrenner. In Bradbury, A. and Swailes, R. (Eds.), *Early Childhood Theories Today.* London: Learning Matters.

Grimmer, T. (2022b) *Supporting Behaviour and Emotions in the Early Years: Strategies and Ideas for Early Years Educators.* Abingdon: Routledge.

Grimmer, T. (2021) *Developing a Loving Pedagogy in the Early Years: How Love Fits with Professional Practice.* Abingdon: Routledge.

Knudsen, E. (2004) Sensitive periods in the development of the brain and behavior. *Journal of Cognitive Neuroscience,* 16(8), pp. 1412–1125.

Liebschner, J. (1992) *A Child's Work. Freedom and Guidance in Froebel's Educational Theory and Practice.* Cambridge, MA: Lutterworth Press.

Lilley, I. (1967) *Friedrich Froebel: A Selection from His Writings.* Cambridge, MA: Cambridge University Press.

Maslow, A. (1943) A theory of human motivation. *Psychological Review,* 50(4), pp. 370–396.

Maslow, A. (1970) *Motivation and Personality* (2nd edn.). New York, NY: Harper & Row.

McWayne, C., Hyun, S., Diez, V. and Mistry, J. (2022) 'We feel connected. . . . And like we belong': A parent-led, staff supported model of family engagement in early childhood. *Early Childhood Education Journal,* 50, pp. 445–457.

Montessori, M. (1942) Maria Montessori: how it all began introduction to the Montessori way. Excerpt from her talk marking the anniversary of the first House of Children. Available at: https://www.montessori.org/maria-montessori-how-it-all-began-introduction-to-the-montessori-way/ (accessed 6 January 1942).

Play England (2020) *Charter for Play.* Available at: https://www.playengland.org.uk/charter-for-play

Play Scotland (2023) *Article 31 of the United Nations Convention on the Rights of the Child.* Available at: https://www.playscotland.org

Shanker, S. (2016) *What Is Shanker Self-Reg?* Available at: www.self-reg.ca/self-reg

Thompson, P. and **Simmons, H.** (2023) *Partnership with Parents in Early Childhood Today.* London: Learning Matters.

UNICEF (1989) *United Nations Convention on the Rights of the Child.* Available at: https://www.unicef.org.uk/what-we-do/un-convention-child-rights/

World Health Organization, UNICEF and the World Bank Group (2018) *The Nurturing Care Framework for Early Childhood Development.* Available at: https://nurturing-care.org/about/what-is-the-nurturing-care-framework/

Zeedyk, S. (2012) *Babies Come into the World Already Connected to Other People.* Available at: http://www.suzannezeedyk.com/wp-content/uploads/2016/03Suzanne-Zeedyk-Babies-Connected-v2.pdf

Zeedyk, S. (2013) *Sabre Tooth Tigers and Teddy Bears: The Connected Baby Guide to Understanding Attachment.* Dundee: Suzanne Zeedyk.

4

LOVE LANGUAGES AND NURTURING TOUCH

AIMS OF THE CHAPTER

1. To understand what constitutes nurturing touch.
2. To recognise the importance of touch and how research confirms this.
3. To acknowledge that children give and receive love in different ways and this can be described as love languages.
4. To use nurturing touch confidently within safeguarding and child protection procedures.

KEY DEFINITIONS

Listed below are the key definitions that this chapter will cover.

Love languages	Love languages acknowledge the difference between being loved and feeling loved and describe the ways in which people may feel loved, their love languages (Chapman and Campbell, 2012).
Nurturing touch	When we use touch within our daily practice as part of a warm, loving relationship in order to nurture the child and help them grow and develop, for example, child holding adult's hand, sitting on adult's lap or when adult and child high five each other.
Quality time	Spending quality time with someone involves being totally present with them, focused on them and enjoying their company.
Words of affirmation	Speaking words of affirmation is when we use language to demonstrate our love through terms of endearment, kindness, encouragement and praise.
Acts of service	When we do an act of service, we are doing something for the person we love regardless of whether we enjoy doing this or not, for example, cooking for someone or driving a child to their sports events.

Gifts	When we talk about the giving and receiving of gifts as a love language, we do not necessarily mean buying things. Gifts can include a leaf, a pebble, saving a train ticket for someone!
Safeguarding	This is the term used when we are working together to promote the welfare of children and prevent and stop the risks and experiences of abuse, neglect or harm to children.
Child protection	Child protection is when we focus on protecting individual children identified as being at risk of suffering harm as part of our safeguarding process.

INTRODUCTION

One of the reasons humans crave contact with other humans is about touch. We cannot live our lives without touch. From the handshake greeting in business meeting to the kiss goodbye for family members, many of us use touch on a daily basis without even noticing or realising it.

We would define nurturing touch as when we use touch within our daily practice as part of a warm, loving relationship in order to nurture the child and help them grow and develop. There are many ways that we use nurturing touch every day – for example, if a child is upset we may ask if they need a cuddle, we may hold their hand as we cross the road or respond to their gestures and lift a child into our arms. In addition, we may high-five a child to celebrate an achievement, gently squeeze their shoulder as we walk by to acknowledge their presence or role-play at being the hairdresser. Bergnehr and Cekaite (2018) identify that there are different ways that adults use touch with children. For example, we may use touch to steer a child in a certain direction physically, to comfort or praise a child, to assist them in a task like helping to wipe their face at a mealtime, or sometimes we use touch as an educational tool, for example, touching the child's fingers when counting.

There is a wealth of research which demonstrates how vital touch is for children and adults alike. This chapter explores the different ways we can express love through love languages and focuses in particular on touch. This is an area which many early childhood professionals have reservations about or recognise as a dilemma (Piper and Smith, 2003); however, it is our hope that this chapter will highlight how vitally important touch is and help alleviate some of those concerns.

LOVE LANGUAGES

After reading the work of Chapman and Campbell (2012), we were challenged to think about the difference between *being* loved and *feeling* loved. Most of us, hopefully all of us, are loved; however, not everyone feels loved. This is because we might feel loved in different ways, for example, one person might feel really loved if they received a bouquet of flowers, whereas another person may dislike the extravagance of such a gift but feel really loved if someone choose to spend quality time with them. In the context of a parent–child relationship, a parent may love their child and tell them frequently they are loved; however, if, in order to feel loved, the child needed kisses and cuddles from their parent, despite *being* loved they may not *feel* loved.

Chapman and Campbell refer to this concept as love languages (2012). They propose that there are five love languages:

1. Words of affirmation
2. Quality time
3. Gifts
4. Acts of service
5. Positive touch.

It is interesting to consider their work within the context of early childhood education: if we can find out children's love languages, we can speak this language, better relate to them and help them to feel loved. We can add identifying their love languages to our toolbox of interaction strategies.

Part of the concept of love languages is imagining that we all have emotional cups or tanks, and during the course of our daily lives, they get filled or emptied depending on our experiences. Some children will arrive in our schools and settings with a half empty or nearly empty emotional cup before they even start the day. It is our job to fill their emotional cup so that they have enough reserves to cope with everything the day throws at them. When children have an empty emotional cup, we may see this as challenging behaviour, for example, in attention-seeking (attachment-seeking – see Chapter 6), fighting or overly competitive or controlling behaviour, or when children are bouncing off the walls, or really quiet and withdrawn. Chapman and Campbell suggest that speaking a child's love language helps to fill their emotional cups (2012) (Figure 4.1).

Figure 4.1   Filling children's emotional cups
Source: Created by Tamsin Grimmer.

We will now consider each of the love languages in turn and explore how we can speak these languages in practice.

WORDS OF AFFIRMATION

We might notice if a child's love language is words of affirmation because this child will probably use words to compliment us or others and tell us they love us, for example, they may say, 'Your hair looks pretty'. 'I love your t-shirt' or 'I love you'. We can reciprocate by using terms of endearment, verbally encouraging our children, showing appreciation, thanking our children, using labelled praise or complimenting them. We are often asked what to do if a child tells an early childhood professional they love them. Our answer is threefold; first, do you love them? It is important to only say I love you if you mean it. . . Second, how might this fit within school or setting policies? In some schools and settings, we would be free to reciprocate and say, 'I love you' back, whereas in others, this would be frowned upon. And lastly, what is your relationship with the child? As a childminder, we may feel free to say I love you to a child, but as a class teacher in a primary school, we may feel this may overstep the professional boundary. There are ways of responding that value the child and what they have said that do not necessarily say I love you in return, for example, 'That's made me feel really special, thank you!' or 'Aww, saying I love you is such a kind thing to say to me!' or 'I love looking after you, you make me smile every day and feel really happy'. We could also draw them a heart on a piece of paper and give it to them as a love note.

QUALITY TIME

If a child's love language is quality time, they will want to spend time with us, they will probably try to gain our attention and others may describe them as our shadow! We can choose to spend time with them, respond to their attention-seeking behaviour, recognising it as attachment-seeking (Chapter 6 explores this in more detail) and offer them undivided and focused attention in small groups or on a 1:1 basis. We can also sit next to them at meals and ask them about their lives, interests and fascinations and we can spend time playing with them. In addition, reminiscing about times we have spent together by looking through old floor books, photo albums or learning journeys is a great way of affirming the quality time we have together.

GIFTS

Has a child ever given you a daisy or a pebble in the outdoor area? This is probably a child whose love language is gifts and they are offering you a love token. When we talk about giving and receiving gifts as a love language, it does not only mean bought gifts or gifts that have a high monetary value. Bringing in our used train ticket, or saving a milk bottle top and offering it to a child can be just as valuable to them. One adult found the biggest conker they could and remembering one specific child was collecting them, they brought it into the setting, saying, 'I saw this and thought of you'. When a child gives you a gift or love token, they are actually saying I love you and probably asking do you love me? And when we reciprocate we are saying I love you too. Therefore, it is vitally important that we value the treasures the children give to us, whether it's a dirty-looking stone from our outside area or a hand-crafted sticky creation!

NURSERY CASE STUDY

Child A was frequently bringing in small flowers each morning and wanting to specifically gift these to certain adults. They were picked on his way to

(Continued)

nursery each morning and had continued for a couple of weeks. I had just read the chapter in Tamsin's book regarding 'Gifts of Love' so spoke to the Head of Centre about how we could return the gift to child A. One evening the Head of Centre did so by giving the child a couple of sunflower seeds for him to grow at home. His reaction showed true excitement and appreciation. From that day on, his gifting of flowers to the staff stopped. However, the conversations about the growing sunflowers continued.

It is interesting that once the gifts were reciprocated, Child A in the case study stopped gifting themselves, perhaps this is because they felt loved and no longer needed to ask 'Do you love me?' by presenting staff with flowers? When we notice specific children have a long language of gifts we can hold them in mind, create resources specifically for them or plan the environment with them in mind and reciprocate by giving gifts back.

ACTS OF SERVICE

Acts of service is doing things for the person you love so we may notice a child's love language as acts of service if they always want to help us, or frequently ask for our help, even though we know they can do the task alone. They are actually saying, 'I love you... do you love me?' Although we are supporting children to be independent, sometimes it is totally appropriate to do things for our children, so when a child requests our help, consider if their emotional cup is empty and needs filling and if it does, jump in to help. Although we may be perfectly capable of making ourselves a cup of tea, there are times when it is heavenly to have one made for us! So if we identify that a child's love language is acts of service, we can ask them to help us with tasks, plan to do things specifically for them, weave their favourite activities into our planning and read the story they love, even if we don't like it much!

TOUCH

Touch is one of the love languages which perhaps needs a little more explanation and exploration. Research tells us that, 'Basic human contact is just as central to a child's development as nutrition. Emergent neuroscientific evidence shows that nurturing touch is essential to foster the physical and emotional security that every child needs in order to thrive' (APPG, 2020, p. 6). However, when we use positive and nurturing touch in our practice, it justifiably raises safeguarding and child protection issues which will need to be addressed. In relation to the children, we may notice if a child's love language is touch because they will be the first to give us a cuddle or may often want to sit on our lap, or stroke our leg whilst we tell the story. We can use touch in a reciprocal way with them, always carefully noticing for signs of assent or dissent. We can offer to greet with a hug, or allow them to choose to cuddle up for a story, we can praise by offering a high five, or play games that require physical touch like 'round and round the garden', rough and tumble, thumb wars or clapping games.

REFLECTIVE PRACTICE EXERCISE

How do you demonstrate our love to the children in your care?
When reflecting upon the love languages of your children, can you recognise
   which languages they speak? How do you know?
In what ways do you speak these languages?
How could you speak these languages more?

IMPORTANCE OF TOUCH

Research tells us that there are two types of touch systems – our discriminative system gives us immediate feedback and tells us we have been touched and would therefore warn us to move if we felt pain, and our affective system responds more slowly and explains the emotional connection we feel and depends upon the relationship between the person touching and the person being touched (McGlone et al., 2014).

When you feel loved, your brain releases chemicals which can be referred to as happy hormones or loving chemicals: oxytocin, dopamine, serotonin and endorphins (Watson, 2021), see Figure 4.2. Oxytocin – often called the love hormone – is produced when we are lovingly touched and helps us to bond and build relationships with others. Dopamine is the brain's reward system, linked with our motivation, and helps us to reach goals. Serotonin is our mood stabiliser which contributes to our wellbeing and happiness, and endorphins are natural painkillers which help to relieve stress and block pain.

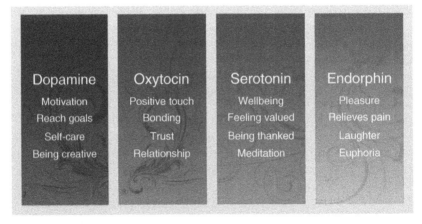

Figure 4.2 Loving chemicals in the brain
Source: Created by Tamsin Grimmer.

Studies have shown the positive impact a loving relationship can have on our health and wellbeing, and oxytocin plays a significant role in this (McGlone et al., 2014). One of the main benefits of oxytocin is that it reduces the stress hormone, cortisol. Cortisol has a regulating effect in our bodies and controls things like our blood sugar levels, which helps to regulate our metabolism. It also has an important role to play in how we respond to stress and, to a certain extent, this is good because it helps us to recognise threats and danger and is part of the freeze, fight or flight survival process. However, too much cortisol or continually high levels of cortisol can lead to toxic stress which, as discussed in Chapter 2, has a detrimental impact on wellbeing into adulthood.

As Figure 4.3 shows, oxytocin also has other positive impacts on our bodies (Gerhardt, 2015; Mainstone-Cotton, 2017). It can improve bonding and social interaction, wellbeing and feelings of calm and help reduce aggression (Ito et al., 2019; McGlone et al., 2014). It also decreases cortisol and stress and stimulates the vagus nerve which helps our bodies to relax faster after experiencing stress (Ito et al., 2019). Oxytocin can also help to reduce anxiety and pain (Eliava et al., 2016), lower blood pressure and reduce our heart rate (Norman et al., 2011). Some studies suggest that oxytocin may also be effective in the prevention of skin ageing (Cho et al., 2019). All these benefits contribute to oxytocin being a very powerful, effective calming influence so it is worth thinking about how we can increase levels of oxytocin.

Figure 4.3   The positive influence of oxytocin
Source: Created by Tamsin Grimmer.

Ways that we can increase oxytocin and other positive chemicals and hormones include:

- building strong attachments with children;
- making eye contact which can help feelings of intimacy;
- hugs and cuddles;
- other positive touch, for example, high five, ruffle hair and squeeze shoulder;

- using love languages, for example, giving gifts, doing an act of kindness for someone, saying loving things and spending time together;
- listening to music and singing along together;
- positive social interactions with others, for example, playing together and cuddling up for a story;
- calming strategies, mindfulness, yoga and meditation;
- stroking a pet;
- having hair played with or brushed (be aware that this can be seen as an intimate act and there are some cultural sensitivities with regard to hair type or style);
- being exposed to natural sunlight (vitamin D promotes oxytocin);
- eating fruits and vegetables (vitamin C and magnesium give us oxytocin);
- eating other foods like dark chocolate (not recommended in our settings!).

For children, one of the main ways that oxytocin is released is in knowing their main carer is close, hearing their voice and being lovingly touched by them. This is why skin-to-skin contact is so important, particularly for newborn babies (Uvnäs-Moberg et al., 2020; Vittner et al., 2018). 'Kangaroo care' is the term given to carrying babies and keeping them as close to a parent as much as possible, often in a skin-to-skin fashion. Research shows this soothes and calms children and is a World Health Organization recommendation for shortening hospital stays for babies born prematurely (WHO, 2015).

In early childhood settings, we are less likely to engage in skin-to-skin contact than a parent; however, research also demonstrates that carrying children is the 'biological norm', that is, humans have been carrying for millions of years so it is part of our evolutionary heritage (Berecz et al., 2020). There are numerous benefits of this for both the child and carer from contributing to secure attachments and improved language skills for the child to enabling the adult to continue with their day-to-day activities whilst remaining close to the child (Bigelow and Williams, 2020; Williams and Turner, 2020). In addition, moving around whilst holding a child has a very calming effect on them (Berecz et al., 2020). Sometimes called 'baby wearing' (Knowles, 2016), many childminders choose to use slings or other baby carriers as part of their everyday practice and more and more nursery and preschool providers are incorporating these tools to enhance their practice with babies and young children.

USING SLINGS AND CARRIERS – CASE STUDIES

In our preschool, we were supporting a child who needed additional support in the setting. We noticed that she was calmer when she was being held. With this in mind, we invested in a sling (baby carrier) so that her key person could hold her so that she felt close to an adult, whilst the adult wasn't restricted in playing or supporting the other children by always carrying her.

Whilst childminding a very young baby, I used a sling wrap, which I'd first used with my own daughter. I found it provided the close, loving feeling of being held for the baby, but also allowed me to engage with the other children or collect from school easily as my hands were freer.

Harlow's research projects from the past, although they make uncomfortable reading due to their questionable ethics or animal cruelty, add context and knowledge to our understanding of the importance of touch and comfort (Harlow, 1958; Harlow and Zimmermann, 1958; Harlow et al., 1965) and the negative implications and poor health outcomes that arise if close physical contact is not present. There is a wealth of research which confirms how touch impacts our emotional and social wellbeing (Field, 2010; von Mohr et al., 2017). Additional findings have identified that social and affective touch were important to both brain development and sensory processing, particularly for newborn babies (Tuulari et al., 2019).

In addition to hugs and cuddles producing oxytocin, research shows that less intimate touch also has a big impact on us, even from strangers. For example, if a person waiting at a table casually touches the arm of their customer, research shows they will be given a higher tip (Hornik, 1992) and if someone asks us for something, we will be more compliant to requests made, which are accompanied by touch (Kleinke, 1977). Guéguen (2004) found that when students were briefly touched on the forearm, they were more likely to volunteer in the classroom. Several studies have found these sorts of results, from a customer in a shop whose hand was briefly touched whilst giving them change, remembering the shop keeper more, and the librarian who touched the hand of the borrower whilst returning their library card made the borrower feel more positive about their library experience. There are ethical considerations here, if touch is indeed this powerful, it could be used to manipulate or coerce someone, particularly children who are more vulnerable. Therefore, we must ensure we are aware of how we use touch and avoid using it to manipulate a child.

CULTURAL DIFFERENCES IN TOUCH

Whilst researching touch I (Tamsin) was struck by one particular study from the 1960s which highlighted cultural differences in conversational touch. Nicknamed the 'coffee shop' research, the researcher Sidney Jourard observed how many times two friends touched each other during a typical conversation in a café (Jourard, 1966). In England, the friends didn't touch each other at all during a whole hour together, and in the United States, they only touched twice, whereas in France, they touched each other 110 times and in Puerto Rico 180 times in the same time frame! This research has been critiqued and questioned as Dutton et al. replicated Jourard's research in several US cities and concluded it would be nearly impossible to record over 100 touches in an hour, since it would be very difficult to determine where one touch ends and another begins (Dutton et al., 2017). Despite these criticisms, it is clear that there are cultural differences in the way touch is used on a daily basis and we need to take this into account with our children in our settings.

Whilst delivering training about developing a loving pedagogy, we often discuss how people from different cultures may have differing practices in relation to touch and attendees share their lived experiences. For example, a colleague from Brazil shared how they use touch all the time in general conversation and in practice with the children, a French colleague shared how they greet by kissing on both cheeks at least once and the child is expected to kiss the adult first, and another colleague from Thailand shared how they greet everyone by pressing their hands together and bowing slightly in a similar pose to the Indian 'Namaste'. A colleague who grew up in New Zealand shared that in Māori culture, the head is viewed as sacred and therefore we should avoid touching another person's head. With so many variations within cultures, and bearing in mind we are living in a multicultural society, it would be helpful to incorporate questions about touch into our settling in discussions with families. This will ensure that we are aware of, and sensitive to, any cultural differences in how touch is used.

REFLECTIVE PRACTICE EXERCISE

You might like to replicate Jourard's research yourself! Sit in a coffee shop or cafeteria and watch people who are eating together. Count how many times one person touches the other as they engage in conversation. If possible, observe people from different cultures to see if you observe any cultural differences. If you live in an area which is not very culturally diverse, this is the perfect excuse to go travelling!

TOUCH AND MEMORY

We often think of touch as a fleeting thing. If we think about touching something like an object, for example, the sensation is there when touching it, and when we are touching it we are as close as we can get to it, having skin contact with it; however, once we let go or move away the sensation has gone. Whereas if we are using a sense like sight, we can look at an object for as long as distance and our eyesight allows. We do not have to get close to it to see it, therefore it could be argued that it is not as intimate an encounter, but less fleeting. Interestingly, Hutmacher and Kuhbandner studied how touching things leaves a lasting imprint on our memory, leading them to conclude that, 'detailed, durable, long-term memory representations are stored as a natural product of haptic perception' (2018, p. 2031). This means that we have an accurate memory for things we touch.

This has implications for human touch too as we remember those who touch us – both physically and emotionally! It is perhaps not surprising therefore that we use the language of touch when we describe an emotional connection with something or someone, for example, 'I felt really touched that she remembered my birthday!' or 'The film really touched me' or 'Keep in touch'. It would sound ludicrous to use other senses in this way... 'I felt really heard that she remembered my birthday...' or 'The film really smelled me!'

USING NURTURING TOUCH IN PRACTICE

Many early childhood professionals are influenced by their belief that they should act as if they were the child's parent. This includes being physically affectionate towards the children. When I (Tamsin) was conducting my own research, one professional stated, 'We hug children and sit them on our knee, in the same way that we would our own children'. Another said, 'If they need a hug, we'll give them a hug, it's those sorts of things that they might ask their parent for... if they're not there, we'll do our best to step in and support whichever need they have', and a third stated, 'They need you to be there caring for them in place of a parent'.

We must be aware that not everyone will respond to touch in the same way and we cannot assume that all children will like to touch or be touched. Some children will flinch or move away if they think we will touch them and it is vital that we read the signals and seek consent when using nurturing touch in practice. However, many young children naturally gravitate towards holding our hand, or sitting on our lap for a cuddle and it is up to us as professionals to consider what is appropriate positive touch in our settings.

CASE STUDY (CHILDMINDER)

I am childminding alongside looking after my own children and childminding allows for a very close relationship. When we're out and about, I hope that from my interactions, members of the public would not know which child is my biological child and which children I am caring for. I try to treat them all equally and according to their needs while they are with me. I use touch in a number of ways on a daily basis. I change nappies, wipe fingers, faces and noses, hold hands when crossing the road, cuddle up for story time and offer the older children a hug when I collect them from school. Sometimes I use touch to praise children, for example, a high five for being kind to a younger child, or just to acknowledge their presence, for example, ruffling their hair or squeezing their shoulder as I walk past. I work closely with parents and carers and they have seen my warm relationship with the children. I sometimes meet children I used to care for as I collect older ones from school and they often run up to me and voluntarily give me a hug or a kiss! I really miss them when they move on and it's great to see them growing up.

SAFEGUARDING AND CHILD PROTECTION

Obviously being physically tactile with children raises safeguarding issues and, of course, it should; however, we should not allow this to prevent us from being physically close to our children. Piper and Smith (2003) identify there is sometimes a 'moral panic' over touch in childcare settings and schools; however, my own research, based on people working with children under 5 years old, highlighted to me that not all adults are fearful about appropriately touching young children (Grimmer, 2023). It could be argued that this willingness to positively and safely use nurturing touch in practice is evidence that a loving pedagogy is in place. We believe we need to openly discuss touch in our settings and schools and be really clear about how we will use touch to demonstrate love, then write it in our policies and ensure that it is agreed upon by everyone. For some children a high five would be totally appropriate, whereas a cuddle might be totally inappropriate – we need to weigh this up and make these decisions case by case.

How we use nurturing and positive touch when working with children may depend on a number of variables: your role in your school or setting, your relationship to the child and the policies of the provision. For example, when I (Tamsin) was a reception class teacher I would have allowed a child to cuddle up for a story or hold my hand at playtime, but I wouldn't have blown a raspberry on their tummy! Whereas when I was a childminder, blowing a raspberry on their tummy whilst changing a nappy was totally appropriate.

If we work as part of a team, it is vital that we have a whole staff discussion about this and ensure that our policies reflect our approach. Many providers are now choosing to have a relationship or loving pedagogy policy alongside their current policies or to replace 'behaviour management' policies. I believe that policies should explicitly talk about touch and the importance of touch and give examples of how adults will use touch in daily practice. For example, *'When a child is upset, we will comfort them, using touch as appropriate, for example by offering them a cuddle'*. A whole school/setting approach is best. Talk in detail about how nurturing touch will be used and agree on the specifics about what constitutes appropriate physical touch in the setting. This can then inform policy. We always suggest discussing specific cases, for example, if a child is allowed to sit on an adult's lap, should they sit on one knee, two knees, with their back to you or fully straddle the adult front to front? What about kissing, do we avoid kissing in the setting, or blow kisses, or engage in 'air' kisses, or cheek kisses? Do we kiss children's hurts better or rub them better? The more specific and detailed we can be in our discussions, the more transparent our policy will be and the more we will avoid any misunderstandings and ensure everyone is clear about where we will draw the lines. In addition, all staff will be acting in line with the policy. This may differ from provision to provision as it will depend on the staff, the children, the views of the parents and any policies already in place.

In addition to having a policy in place, settings will also want to ensure their supervision arrangements are effective and offer an opportunity for staff to share any safeguarding concerns and there are whistleblowing procedures in place. This is also about staff feeling free to raise any concerns or discuss sensitive issues with their supervisor. This relies on building honest and trusting relationships between staff members and adopting a loving pedagogy and nurturing ethos is helpful in ensuring this is in place.

CONSENT

There appears to be very little research exploring consent around touch which doesn't explicitly talk about sexual consent; however, teaching consent from an early age is vital. Consent is about a child giving permission to be touched or agreeing for something to happen to them. Children need to learn that their bodies belong to them and they can set boundaries regarding this. Therefore, seeking consent around touch is particularly important and can set the tone for life.

We need to model this and encourage parents to also develop a culture of consent. This can begin from birth, for example, asking a child 'Can I change your nappy?' This might sound a little strange because babies cannot give verbal consent or respond to this sort of question, but this is about engaging in respectful communication with children and part and parcel of a loving pedagogy. Asking a child for consent will also involve teaching children the serve and return of conversation, so we might say, 'I'm going to change your nappy now, is that OK?' and then wait a moment before carrying on, 'Come on then, let's go to the changing table...' The idea is to make eye contact, acknowledge them and include them in the process and experience, rather than simply do things to them.

When we talk about young children giving consent, we often use the term 'assent' because, generally speaking, young children are unable to fully understand what they are consenting to. Therefore, it is the role of the educator to look for signs of assent, or agreement, by observing children's body language, what they say and their behaviour. We need to actively listen and notice whether or not they consent to nurturing touch. It's also important to remember about consent if children are meeting other adults, including family members. We may need to educate others and introduce ideas around boundaries and consent to parents and carers and role model asking for consent in the presence of parents, for example, on arrival and pick up. . . 'Shall we wave goodbye or would you like a hug goodbye?'

REFLECTIVE PRACTICE EXERCISE

Invite a colleague to observe you at several different points during the day. Ask them to note if you are using touch with colleagues, children or others and record context and details about the experience. Once you have gathered this information reflect upon how you and the children are using touch. What can you learn from this?

Time	Context	Who	Details
8.30 am	Child arrived at setting	LB (child)	Adult welcomed child with arms outstretched. LB, smiling, ran into her embrace.
8.45 am	During welcome activities	Small group	No touch. Adult sitting at table with 4 children.
9.00 am	Whole group story	Whole group SH in particular	SH sitting by adult's feet, stroking adult's leg during story. Adult reached down and gently squeezed SH's shoulder.

CONCLUSION

There is no one single way to demonstrate love to another person: we all give and receive love in different ways as Chapman and Campbell's (2012) work around love languages suggests. As early childhood professionals, part of our role is to find out the love languages of our children and then speak and use these languages to enable our children to feel loved. We believe this will empower children and ultimately help them to feel safe and secure and therefore they will be ready to learn (Grimmer, 2021).

One of the love languages we will observe is touch. Many children (and adults) will feel loved when lovingly touched or when touch is used on a daily basis. Using nurturing touch is not without its problems or dilemmas; however, in the light of the wealth of research highlighting the positive impact touch can have, we should not let any safeguarding or child protection fears prevent us from using touch positively (Byrne, 2016). We should stand firm in our policy and practices, knowing that children's lives will be enhanced by our loving interactions with them.

KEY QUESTIONS

1. How do you use nurturing touch in practice?
2. Have you recognised any love languages in your key children?
3. What might you say to reassure a parent who is concerned about your use of touch in the setting?

References

All- Party Parliamentary Group on a Fit and Healthy Childhood (APPG) (2020) *Wellbeing and Nurture: Physical and Emotional Security in Childhood.* Available at: https://fhcappg.org.uk/wp-content/uploads/2020/07/ReportWellbeinga ndNurtureFinal140720.pdf

Berecz, B., Cyrilleb, M., Casselbrantc, U., Oleksakd, S. and **Norholte, H.** (2020) Carrying human infants – An evolutionary heritage. *Infant Behavior and Development,* p. 60.

Bergnehr, D. and **Cekaite, A.** (2018) Adult-initiated touch and its functions at a Swedish preschool: Controlling, affectionate, assisting and educative haptic conduct. *International Journal of Early Years Education,* 26(3), pp. 312–331.

Bigelow, A. and **Williams, L.** (2020) To have and to hold: Effects of physical contact on infants and their caregivers. *Infant Behavior and Development,* p. 61.

Byrne, J. (2016) Love in social care: Necessary pre-requisite or blurring of boundaries. *Scottish Journal of Residential Child Care,* 15(3), pp. 152–158.

Chapman, G. and **Campbell, R.** (2012) *The 5 Love Languages of Children.* Chicago, IL: Northfield Publishing.

Cho, S., Kim, A., Kim, J., Choi, D., Son, E. and **Shin, D.** (2019) Oxytocin alleviates cellular senescence through oxytocin receptor-mediated extracellular signal-regulated kinase/Nrf2 signalling. *British Journal of Dermatology,* 181(6), pp. 1216–1225.

Dutton, J., Johnson, A. and **Hickson, M.** (2017) Touch revisited: Observations and methodological recommendations. *Journal of Mass Communication and Journalism,* 7, p. 5.

Eliava, M., Melchior, M., Knobloch-Bollmann, H., Wahis, J., da Silva Gouveia, M., Tang, Y., Cristian Ciobanu, A., Triana del Rio, R., Roth, L., Althammer, F., Chavant, V., Goumon, Y., Gruber, T., Petit-Demoulière, N., Busnelli, M., Chini, B., Tan, L., Mitre, M., Froemke, R., Chao, M., Giese, G., Sprengel, R., Kuner, R., Poisbeau, P., Seeburg, P., Stoop, R., Charlet, A. and **Grinevich, V.** (2016) A new population of parvocellular oxytocin neurons controlling magnocellular neuron activity and inflammatory pain processing. *Neuron,* 89(6), pp. 1291–1304.

Field, T. (2010) Touch for socioemotional and physical well-being: A review. *Developmental Review,* 30(4), pp. 367–383.

Gerhardt, S. (2015) *Why Love Matters: How Affection Shapes a Baby's Brain* (2nd edn.). Hove: Routledge.

Grimmer, T. (2021) *Developing a Loving Pedagogy: How Love Fits with Professional Practice.* Abingdon: Routledge.

Grimmer, T. (2023) Is there a place for love in an early childhood setting? *Early Years: An International Research Journal.*

Guéguen, N. (2004) Nonverbal encouragement of participation in a course: The effect of touching. *Social Psychology of Education,* 7, pp. 89–98.

Harlow, H. (1958) The nature of love. *American Psychologist*, 13, pp. 673–685.

Harlow, H. and Zimmermann, R. (1958) The development of affectional responses in infant monkeys. *Proceedings of the American Philosophical Society*, 102, pp. 502–509.

Harlow, H., Dodsworth, R. and Harlow, M. (1965) Total social isolation in monkeys. *Proceedings of the National Academy of Sciences of the United States of America*. 54(1), pp. 90–97.

Hornik, J. (1992) Tactile stimulation and consumer response. *Journal of Consumer Research*, 19, pp. 449–458.

Hutmacher, F. and Kuhbandner, C. (2018) Long-term memory for haptically explored objects: Fidelity, durability, incidental encoding, and cross-modal transfer. *Psychological Science*, 29(12), pp. 2031–2038.

Ito, E., Shima, R. and Yoshioka, T. (2019) A novel role of oxytocin: Oxytocin-induced well-being in humans. *Biophysics and Physicobiology*, 24(16), pp. 132–139.

Jourard, S. (1966) An exploratory study of body-accessibility. *British Journal of Social & Clinical Psychology*, 5, pp. 221–231.

Kleinke, C. (1977) Compliance to requests made by gazing and touching experimenters in field settings. *Journal of Experimental Social Psychology*, 13(3), pp. 218–223.

Knowles, R. (2016) *Why Babywearing Matters*. London: Pinter & Martin Ltd.

Mainstone-Cotton, S. (2017) *Promoting Young Children's Emotional Health and Wellbeing: A Practical Guide for Professionals and Parents*. London: Jessica Kingsley Publishers.

McGlone, F., Wessberg, J. and Olausson, H. (2014) Discriminative and affective touch: Sensing and feeling, *Neuron*, 82(4), pp. 737–755.

von Mohr, M., Kirsch, L. P. and Fotopoulou, A. (2017) The soothing function of touch: Affective touch reduces feelings of social exclusion. *Scientific Reports*, 7, p. 13516.

Norman, G., Cacioppo, J., Morris, J., Malarkey, W., Berntson, G. and Devries, A. (2011) Oxytocin increases autonomic cardiac control: Moderation by loneliness. *Biological Psychology*, 86(3), pp. 174–180.

Piper, H. and Smith, H. (2003). 'Touch' in educational and child care settings: Dilemmas and responses. *British Educational Research Journal*, 29(6), pp. 879–894.

Tuulari, J., Scheinin, N., Lehtola, S., Merisaari, H., Saunavaara, J., Parkkola, R., Sehlstedt, I., Karlsson, L., Karlsson, H. and Björnsdotter, M. (2019) Neural correlates of gentle skin stroking in early infancy. *Developmental Cognitive Neuroscience*, 35, pp. 36–41.

Uvnäs-Moberg, K., Handlin, L. and Petersson, M. (2020) Neuroendocrine mechanisms involved in the physiological effects caused by skin-to-skin contact – With a particular focus on the oxytocinergic system. *Infant Behavior and Development*, p. 61.

Vittner, D., McGrath, J., Robinson,J., Lawhon, G., Cusson, R., Eisenfeld, L., Walsh, S., Young, E. and Cong, X. (2018) Increase in oxytocin from skin-to-skin contact enhances development of parent–infant relationship. *Biological Research For Nursing*, 20(1), pp. 54–62.

Watson, S. (2021) Feel-good hormones: How they affect your mind, mood and body. Available at: https://www.health.harvard.edu/mind-and-mood/feel-good-hormones-how-they-affect-your-mind-mood-and-body

Williams, L. and Turner, P. (2020) Infant carrying as a tool to promote secure attachments in young mothers: Comparing intervention and control infants during the still-face paradigm. *Infant Behavior and Development*, p. 58.

World Health Organization (2015) *WHO Recommendations on Interventions to Improve Preterm Birth Outcomes*. Geneva: World Health Organization.

5

LOVE AND NURTURE BEYOND THE SETTING

AIMS OF THE CHAPTER

1. To explore holistic and therapeutic support for children and families.
2. To recognise the importance of building relationships with families and developing loving and nurturing relationships with parents and carers.
3. To develop a whole setting approach and ethos of nurturing care.
4. To explore family support and how this can develop a culture of nurture within early years settings.

KEY DEFINITIONS

Listed below are the key definitions that this chapter will cover.

Belonging	To belong, one must have an established relationship or connection with a group of people. It is possible for children to be emotionally strong, self-assured and able to deal with challenges and difficulties when they feel a sense of belonging and pride in themselves and their families, their peers and their communities.
Parent partnership	Parent partnership involves early childhood professionals developing responsive and reciprocal relationships in which power is shared. Genuine partnership occurs when teachers and families collaborate in making provision decisions about children's learning.
Infant massage	Infant massage is a lovely way to enjoy time with a baby and it can also help with developing a bond.
Attachment	Attachment refers to a deep and enduring emotional bond that connects one person to another across time and space.
Family support	Through family support, families can access a wide range of support and services, including formal and informal supports (such as parent-to-parent connections) as well as a community system of services designed to support the wellbeing of families and children.

INTRODUCTION

Typically, early childhood texts focus on activities and approaches that take place within the setting. The concept of nurture and love, however, extends much further than this. In developing and extending our early childhood settings, parents and carers play an essential role. It is the purpose of this chapter to explore how love and nurture can extend our practice by establishing a relationship with parents and carers promoting children's development and how this supports a child's sense of self. This chapter will discuss the importance of supporting children and families holistically, as well as identifying any needs parents and caregivers may have to support them and their children. In this chapter, we will examine how we can provide aspects of family support to ensure a child feels loved and is nurtured holistically.

Professionals in the early years provide parents and caregivers with valuable opportunities to interact with them daily. According to research, if parents and carers are actively involved in their children's learning and activities in school or early childhood settings, children are more likely to thrive both academically and in terms of their general wellbeing (Desforges and Aboucher, 2003; Field, 2010; Hunt et al., 2011). Children can be supported more effectively to reach their full potential when a systemic approach is taken, in which families, early childhood professionals and support colleagues work together.

WHERE DOES IT ALL BEGIN?

As early childhood professionals, we should consider not only our own education experiences but also those of our parents and caregivers as well. Taking into consideration the experiences of parents and caregivers going through education can have a significant impact on their relationship with you and the setting.

REFLECTIVE PRACTICE EXERCISE

Thinking about the parents within your setting:

How did they experience education?
Did they find the environment challenging?
Did they have a negative experience or a positive one?
Did the adults around them have low or high expectations for them?

CASE STUDY

Maria has decided to go back to work after having nine months off as part of her maternity package. Her baby daughter Niamh will be starting Playdays Nursery soon and she wants to see how Niamh is going to get on without her

(Continued)

being around. Niamh is a content baby but has only experienced her mother and extended family. Maria has taken Niamh to baby massage classes which she enjoys and play time at the local church. Maria has asked for a meeting prior to baby Niamh starting nursery.

REFLECTIVE QUESTIONS

Starting from the position of Maria and Niamh:

What would be your first priorities?
What insights would you want to know before they start?
How would you ease some of the apprehensive feelings that the mother has before Niamh starts attending your setting?

As the case study outlines above, children and their parents share a special relationship that should be nurtured and cherished. To support this, we must not only love and nurture the child in our care but also explain to the parent how we will care for their child. Your family background, your academic background and your cultural and personal beliefs about education may all have a profound impact on how parents and caregivers view you and the early childhood setting. Apart from early childhood education, parents may feel that they are constantly being scrutinised for the quality of their parenting due to issues relating to healthcare and social services. This scrutiny can also be felt and experienced by the child. I believe that it is important to emphasise that most parents are concerned about what is best for their children. It is important to be aware that for some parents, speaking with an early years professional or teacher may be a stressful experience.

By building a positive relationship with parents and caregivers, you will be able to better understand the child's context and advocate for the child if additional support is required. Your approach to building these relationships is extremely important, and the interactions you have will support your position that the child and their needs is at the centre of the partnership. It is a central principle of the Early Years Foundation Stage Statutory Framework (DFE, 2024) that children should develop strong relationships with their parents at an early age. This is especially important since they may be leaving their parents for the first time in their lives to attend an early years setting. One of the most recent acknowledgements that parents play the most significant role in their children's development and wellbeing is the document *The Best Start for Life: A Vision for the 1,001 Critical Days* (Department for Health and Social Care, 2021).

All aspects of a child's development are affected by their relationships. Children learn about themselves and the world through their relationships with their parents, family members and caregivers. Children benefit from relationships because they can express themselves – a cry, a laugh or a question – and receive something in return – a cuddle, a smile or an answer. The information children 'receive back' provides them with important information about what the world is like as well as how to act in that world – how to think, understand, communicate, behave, show emotions and develop social skills.

When you respond to a baby or child's babble or cuddle request in a warm, loving and gentle way, you help them learn about communication, behaviour and emotions. You're also building a strong relationship between you and the child and help them feel safe and secure when you respond warmly to their needs. By doing this, a child will feel more confident to explore the world when they feel safe and attached to you.

All these interactions with a child develop their confidence, resilience and communication skills. In adolescence and adulthood, a child will need these skills to cope with problems, deal with stress and form healthy relationships. A child is also more likely to have better mental health and fewer behavioural challenges if they have strong attachments and relationships early in life. Building a warm, positive and responsive relationship with a child and parents/families now benefits them for the rest of their lives, and you're shaping the adult they will become.

ARE WE A SETTING THAT IS OUTWARD FACING?

Many of our families come from the community where our early years building sits, so this section of the chapter is an opportunity for us to think about how we are engaging with the wider community so that we are offering the best possible start to our children within our settings.

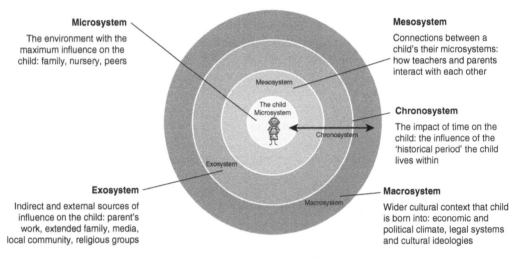

Figure 5.1   Ecological systems model (Grimmer, 2022)
Source: Based on Bronfenbrenner (1979).

One way to see how we can look at positioning the child and enhancing how we are being outward facing is by using the ecological systems theory model developed by Bronfenbrenner (1979) (Figure 5.1). The environment has a significant impact on a child's development according to Bronfenbrenner's ecological systems theory. In Bronfenbrenner's model, the environment is represented by a series of systems that influence a child's development directly or indirectly. Therefore, a child's development is influenced by their biology and their environment. In the classroom or setting, Bronfenbrenner's ecological systems theory can be applied in many ways. It is possible for parents and early childhood professionals to maintain open, respectful communication, and for educators to be aware and sensitive to the exosystems and macrosystems that can affect a child's development.

In Bronfenbrenner's ecological systems theory, the exosystem is represented by how the larger world affects the child's microsystem. As the child's microsystem is populated by people who impact the child on a daily basis (for example, parents, siblings, educators and peers), any action taken by the exosystem indirectly impacts the child. The development of a child can be adversely affected if that impact is significant.

By reflecting on clear outcomes for our children and using the rings of Bronfenbrenner model to see what is impacting them, or the value of the impact, we can support nurture and love for children within the community. Using the model in Chapter 2, think about how you could evaluate your setting to support love and nurture and getting to know more about where the children are coming from in the following ways:

- Utilising team meetings for reflection.
- Valuing a play-based pedagogy.
- Auditing resources.
- Video from a child's height and perspective – what do they see? (This can be done with a mobile phone, an iPad or a GoPro. Please use equipment provided from within your setting rather than using your own.)
- Are you outward facing?
- Are you questioning your own values and beliefs and finding out more about the children in your care?

HOW TO DEVELOP NURTURE AND LOVE THROUGH PARENT WORKSHOPS – BABY AND INFANT MASSAGE

It is common for settings to offer support to parents so that the offer of nurture and love between the setting, the child and the parents is strengthened. Developing nurturing through touch is one way to do so. In our early childhood settings, baby massage can be a useful implementation to use. Many cultures see infant massage as a tradition that begins immediately after birth, and it is described as a structured touch of the skin (Mrljak et al., 2022). Performing infant massage differs worldwide in terms of duration, intensity, extent, use of oil and parental involvement.

The development of a child during infancy occurs rapidly (Stern, 2018). According to Bowlby (1979), attachment begins at birth. A child and their mother interact; the mother reacts to the child's signals and adapts their behaviour, and over time, the child learns to respond to their mother's behaviour. A study found that mothers who learnt and performed infant massage during a hospital stay experienced reduced anxiety and a stronger attachment to their children (Gürol and Polat, 2012). According to Bowlby's theory, a good parent–child attachment is important and entails that a child feels safe, yielding better conditions for development and exploration.

To strengthen the nurturing relationship, infant massage is a good way to develop a stronger bond between yourself as the professional, the parent and the child. It is well known that infant massage improves mothers' mental wellbeing (Garmy, 2012) and reduces anxiety, depression and stress (Galanakis et al., 2015).

You could deliver baby/infant massage within your settings, allowing parents to join in and develop those holistic health and development benefits. One of the companies that puts infant massage at the forefront of development is the Developmental Baby Massage Centre (link is in the References), which was founded by Peter Walker, a well-respected teacher of Developmental Baby Massage who has been practising Developmental Baby Massage for babies and children since the 1980s onwards. Becoming a trained Developmental Baby Massage teacher will allow you to practice as an instructor to support children and parents with some of the outcomes discussed in the research above.

REFLECTIVE POINT

Developmental Baby Massage – Written by Peter Walker (2023).

> *Peter Walker is the world's foremost authority on baby massage. A trained physical therapist, he offers a certificated teacher training course in baby massage directed at midwives, health visitors, neonatal nurses as well as parents. He has written a number of books on the subject.*

Massage Movement and Development. The foundational elements of a child's upright posture, movement and mobility are intricately woven into the achievement of locomotor milestones. For parents, grasping the significance of these milestones, their sequential progression and the advantages they offer is of utmost importance.

While it's only natural for parents to eagerly anticipate their child's developmental progress, it is vital to underscore that the speed of attainment is not the primary concern. Rather, our focus should be on 'how well, not quickly' a child performs these.

The pace at which a child acquires skills like sitting, crawling, standing and walking is less significant than the thoroughness with which they master these abilities. Therefore, it is imperative not to overlook the significance of each milestone in their developmental journey and allocate sufficient time for practice.

Through consistent practice and cognitive mapping, a child can attain the independence necessary to lift and control their head, sit upright, use their arms and hands, stand and walk with proficiency and confidence. Much of this process revolves around the timely enablement of sections of the spine and the child's early relationship with gravity.

For children who face or are at risk of disability/disabilities such as those with conditions like cerebral palsy, Prader–Willi syndrome or spina bifida. Early intervention, rooted in an understanding of the motor milestones and

(Continued)

the regular practice of appropriate tactile methods, can have a profound, beneficial effect on the motor development of these children.

In conclusion, the journey of a child's development is marked by milestones that play a critical role in their overall wellbeing. Children with developmental challenges benefit permanently from early interventions based on a solid understanding of these milestones and the correct approach based upon 'massage and movement'. For all parents, comprehending the significance of these milestones, their sequential order and the advantages they offer is of paramount importance.

KEY COMPONENTS ON HOW TO BUILD A POSITIVE RELATIONSHIP WITH PARENTS

The main way to include parents and build positive relationships is to make time to listen to them. Here are a few other suggestions which may support in building those relationships to foster more emphasis on love and nurture within your early years setting.

- Try and organise face-to-face contact with parents to avoid making assumptions about what it is we think parents want to know.
- Make time to use opportunities to involve parents in their children's learning.
- Invite parents into the setting to share their skills, experiences and interests, including offering support to parents where this is needed.
- Invite parents to organise social events, workshops and even access training and volunteering schemes.
- Share both professional and parent knowledge of the child's development and learning.
- Develop classes and workshops which allow parents to learn, develop and gain a greater understanding of the principles embedded by the setting.

There is an element of empowerment for parents when their views and interests, as well of those of their children, are being valued by professionals. This can be the start of a positive relationship between the setting and parents for positive outcomes of their children. However, these relationships are not something that is formed quickly, and professionals need to recognise that the above is something to aim for over a longer period of time, when both parents and professionals truly value the expertise of each other and maintaining the sole focus on the child.

Birth to 5 Matters: Non-statutory Guidance for the Early Years Foundation Stage Curriculum (Early Years Coalition, 2021, p. 29) states that 'parents need to be seen as key partners' and makes the following key points:

- Parents make a crucial difference to children's outcomes.
- Parents are children's first and most enduring educators.
- Each unique family must be welcomed and listened to.
- Consider levels of engagement to make the most of relating to parents.
- Practitioners have a responsibility to work with all families.
- Clear leadership regarding partnership with parents will provide the right foundation.

Each family and child should be seen as unique which embodies the core value of nurture and love. Creating a welcoming atmosphere should be evident from the moment a visit is made regarding their child. We hear a lot about how settings have created a welcoming and inclusive environment. My mum (Aaron) has always said, 'You know how loving and warm a place is by how they greet you and make you welcome'. I would have to agree with my mum here. It is all about creating those first impressions – for the children, for the parents and visitors. It is essential that all families feel that they belong.

An early childhood professional's attitude and the language and communication methods used, as well as the environment and resources available, are all indicative of this. After the setting has been selected and confirmed, the key person's role includes establishing relationships with families. Developing relationships with extended families and the child's parents is not only a responsibility but also a great privilege. It is important to respect and celebrate the uniqueness of each child and family, as each brings aspects of their own cultural knowledge and values that enrich the environment as a whole.

ATTACHMENT

Attachment is like an invisible thread connecting a baby and young child with the significant adults in their lives, according to Hunt (2022). As a major aspect of early childhood development, love and nurture supports the development of secure attachments, which are vital for emotional wellbeing. In nurturing, 'attachment' is one principle, where children feel a sense of security, as well as an environment in which a caregiver listens and cares unconditionally for them.

In *The Nurturing Parenting Programs*, Dr Stephen J. Bavolek, principal author, recognises nurturing as a critical life skill which can help children become caring, respectful and cooperative adults. According to this, children learn to respect themselves, others and their surroundings when we care for and treat them with respect (Bradbury, 2022).

All aspects of a child's growth, development and behaviour can be affected by their early experiences. As a result of their positive experiences, they develop healthy relationships with peers and adults, strong communication skills, a curiosity to learn new things and a sense of wellbeing. Every aspect of a baby's life is dependent on their primary caregiver. It is the reciprocal relationships and the unconditional love and care they receive that enable them to make sense of the way their world works (Hunt, 2022).

In order to develop intellectually, socially, emotionally and physically, basic physical needs must be met, and a sense of security built. In 1943, Maslow proposed this theory, which is still very relevant today. People are instinctively motivated to fulfil certain needs, according to Maslow. Upon fulfilling one need, a person seeks to fulfil the next (Maslow, 1943) (Figure 5.2).

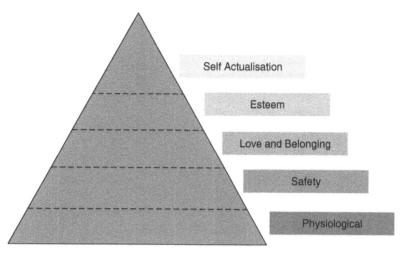

Figure 5.2   Maslow hierarchy of needs. A visual adapted by the authors
Source: Based on Maslow (1943).

It is for this reason that the model is often referred to as a pyramid. If basic needs are not met, then self-actualisation, that is, meeting your potential and being strong, responsive and capable, will not happen.

REFLECTION POINT

There are many ways that parents and caregivers can nurture children and provide secure attachment. Just like building these stones, our children need the approach of love and nurture to build a child's development holistically (Figure 5.3). Some of these may include:

- Assist with physical needs – providing food, clothing and shelter in a safe and comfortable manner. Take care of a child's routine health needs, such as well-child visits and dental care. Find out where help is available for serious health problems in your community.
- Describe how children develop – children develop at their own pace, but the sequence in which they develop is predictable.
- The voice of the child. Be aware of your body language and tone of voice. There is more to communication than just what we say.
- Provide opportunities for a child to explore the wonders of the world. Encourage their curiosity and exploration by providing a variety of age-appropriate toys and activities. Discover a child's interests. Keep in mind that their opinions may differ from yours!
- Provide all children with challenges that encourage independence and self-worth. A two-year-old can pick up toys and place them in a

(Continued)

(Continued)

designated area. Take note of the unique qualities each and every child has and appreciate them for what they are.

- Disciplinary measures should be recognised to teach and guide all children in making appropriate choices. Make sure your teaching is fair, consistent and constructive. Follow through with what you say, mean and do!

- Not all children have to 'like' everything you do. All children will learn that we all make mistakes and that no problem is too big for you to solve together by modelling forgiveness.

- Establish traditions – teach a child about your own family's rituals, celebrations and traditions. Creating new traditions can help you feel like you belong to a larger community, which may include yourfamily, friends and community where the child lives.

- Parenting is not an easy job. It is important that we advocate to all parents that they Take care of themselves To be able to care for the children in their lives, caregivers must take care of their own needs.

- Be willing to listen to parents when they need to ask for help – no one can raise a child alone. To raise a child, it takes a village, extended family, friends, co-workers, neighbours, school and community. When you need assistance, find out where and how to get it.

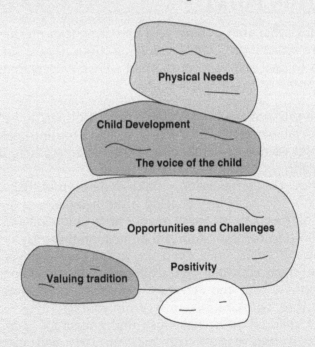

Figure 5.3   The building stones of Love and Nurture for Early Years children

Our early childhood settings place the child at the centre of our practices, working collaboratively with parents and children in order to grow the children we care for. As a result of the points above, we can enable a loving and nurturing approach. The nurturing environment plays a significant role in a child's emotional development and wellbeing, according to Bradbury (2022). Many pioneers in early childhood studied the impact of the child's environment on their development. In the 1800s, Friedrich Froebel discussed an approach that could inspire and guide children's imagination and behaviour. The Reggio Emilia Approach sees the environment as a 'third teacher', following the works of Loris Malaguzzi.

DEVELOPING A SENSE OF FAMILY SUPPORT

Early years settings can be a positive place to develop family support for both the children and parents. Sometimes, parents need that extra support to be able to get through challenges that life throws at them. There is not a manual that tells anyone how to parent or care for their children, and sometimes the need arises for parents to ask for help.

A child's key person within the setting can be a great advocate for providing family support. A strong emotional environment is a place where a child feels safe, cared for and relaxed and is physically and emotionally healthy. Children need to form a close bond and trusting relationship with a Key Person who can ensure that their learning is tailored to meet the needs of the child and also build a relationship alongside parents to be able to do this effectively. By supporting parents when they need that extra guidance or an ear to listen to them allows you to tune into the children's interests and interact with them to support and extend their learning and development, which jointly engages in areas of problem-solving and supporting behaviour.

Parents want the best for their children. They want you to love and nurture their children. They know that children thrive best in an inclusive environment based on mutual respect, where uniqueness is valued. Sometimes parents need a bit of guidance, they may need nurturing too, and fostering a warm and welcoming approach to family support meets the needs of both the children and their families.

Family support is based on positive relationships within early years settings by being:

- Warm and loving, fostering a sense of belonging.
- Sensitive and responsive to the child's needs, feelings and interests.
- Supportive of the child's own efforts and independence.
- Consistent in setting clear boundaries and creating a stimulating environment.

(Development Matters in the EYFS, Early Education, 2012)

Below is a diagram that explores why a sense of belonging focuses on the child NOW, developing a child-centred approach for what children need (see Figure 5.4). By focusing on a child's holistic needs, it portrays a positive picture for their learning and positions their well-being at the centre of their learning and development. We must not fall into the trap of cramming lost learning to catch up, placing more pressure on our children, instead we must focus on the NOW. How do those children and their families need to be supported NOW in order to develop holistically? We are going to explain each aspect of the model we have created so that you can develop this within your practice.

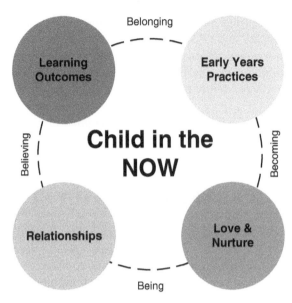

Figure 5.4 The child's sense of belonging in the NOW

First, let us explain how we developed this model. When we think about children, we tend to focus on their learning outcomes; however, other aspects of their development must also be taken into consideration. Providing belonging, becoming, being and believing within our early childhood practice is something we can all do. Let's unpick these in more detail:

Belonging for children: To belong, one must have an established relationship or connection with a group of people. It is possible for children to be emotionally strong, self-assured and able to deal with challenges and difficulties when they feel a sense of belonging and pride in themselves and their families, their peers and their communities.

Becoming: During childhood, children's identities, knowledge, understandings, capacities and skills change. Events and circumstances shape them in many ways. The process of becoming reflects the rapid and significant change that occurs in the early years as children learn and develop.

Being: As with many aspects of development and learning, children don't develop a sense of being on their own. The caregiver and child engage in sensitive, responsive exchanges within them, which grows out of attuned relationships.

Believing: It means many things to believe in a child, including providing a nurturing environment for all children, keeping a child's best interests in mind and providing a child with the opportunities they need to succeed. Even if they don't believe it, you should speak into their inherent goodness, providing a child with choices, and a child should not be exposed to adult insecurities.

Within this model, there are four key principles which we want to make clear why they are at the centre of supporting the child in the NOW moments.

Learning Outcomes

With learning comes a strong sense of identity for the child. Children become connected to their world and contribute to it. This outcome promotes wellbeing and develops a sense of self in the child. Self-confidence and involvement in learning are developed in children. In order to become effective communicators, children need to develop a sense of confidence.

Early Years Practices

Practices in the early years should be holistic, integrated and interconnected. Children's needs must be addressed in our practices and our focus should be on play-based learning. For children's learning environments, developing a pedagogy around play is essential. We need to be sensitive to the cultures and needs of our children. It is important to observe children so that assessments can be based on their development and wellbeing.

Relationships

We need to create a sense of what our children need in the NOW based on their relationships with each other. A sense of love and nurture can only be developed through secure, respectful and reciprocal relationships. In order to raise high expectations for our children, we must respect diversity, develop partnerships, inclusion and respect equity. In order to become effective early childhood professionals, we must be reflective, be critical and think about our ongoing learning.

Love & Nurture

Young children need plenty of emotional and cognitive support, love and nurturing in addition to food, water, shelter, sleep and hygiene. It is important for caregivers to express love and affection to their children every day. By doing so, young children feel safe, comforted and included in a warm, bonded relationship. In fact, children who feel secure are more likely to learn and to develop physically and mentally.

KEY QUESTIONS

1. In what ways can you adopt a loving and nurturing approach with parents and family members?
2. Think about each child in the NOW. Do they feel like that they belong? Do you support them becoming and being? How do you demonstrate that you believe in them?
3. Does your setting include holistic nurturing approaches such as external workshops for parents and children, for example, baby massage?

Further reading and resources

Peter Walker – Baby Massage Teacher Training – http://www.babymassageteachertraining.com/about/

References

Bowlby J. (1979) *The Making & Breaking of Affectional Bonds.* London: Tavistock.

Bradbury, A. (2022) Dr Stephen Bavolek, chapter 1, in **Bradbury, A.** and **Swailes, R.** (Eds.), *Early Childhood Theories Today.* London: Learning Matters.

Bronfenbrenner, U. (1979) *The Ecology of Human Development: Experiments by Nature and Design.* Boston, MA: Harvard University Press.

Department for Education (2024) *Statutory Framework for the early Years Foundation Stage.* Available at: https://www.gov.uk/government/publications/early-years-foundation-stage-framework--2

Department of Health and Social Care (2021) *The Best Start for Life: A Vision for the 1,001 Critical Days.* Available at: https://www.gov.uk/government/publications/the-best-start-for-life-a-vision-for-the-1001-critical-days (accessed on 2 January 2023).

Desforges, C. and Aboucher, A. (2003) *The Impact of Parental Involvement, Parental Support and Family Education on Pupil Achievement and Adjustment: A Literature Review.* DfES Research Report 433.

Early Education (2012) *Development Matters in the Early Years Foundation Stage. (EYFS).* Available at: https://dera.ioe.ac.uk/id/eprint/14042/7/development%20matters%20in%20the%20early%20foundation%20stageRedacted.pdf (accessed on 1 April 2023).

Early Years Coalition (2021) *Birth to Five Matters Non-statutory Guidance to the Early Years Foundation Stage.* Available at: https://birthto5matters.org.uk/wp-content/uploads/2021/03/Birthto5Matters-download.pdf

Field, F. (2010) *The Foundation Years – Preventing Poor Children Becoming Poor Adults.* London: Cabinet Office. Available at: https://webarchive.nationalarchives.gov.uk/ukgwa/20110120090141/http:/povertyreview.independent.gov.uk/media/20254/poverty-report.pdf

Galanakis, M., Ntaouti, E., Tsitsanis, G. and Chrousos, G.P. (2015). The effects of infant massage on maternal Distress: A systematic review. *Psychology,* 6, p. 2091.

Garmy, P. (2012) Aktuellt Kunskapsläge Om Spädbarnsmassage -Systematisk Litteraturöversikt 2006–2011. *Vård I Nord,* 32, pp. 29–33.

Grimmer, T. (2022) Bronfenbrenner, chapter 2. In **Bradbury, A.** and **Swailes, R.** (Eds.), *Early Childhood Theories Today.* London. Learning Matters.

Gürol, A. and Polat, S. (2012) The effects of baby massage on attachment between mother and their infants. *Asian Nursing Research,* 6, pp. 35–41.

Hunt, M. (2022) *Helping Every Child to Thrive in the Early Years: How to Overcome the Effect of Disadvantage.* London: Routledge.

Hunt, S., Virgo, S., Klett-Davies, M., Page, A. and Apps, J. (2011) *Provider Influence on the Early Home Learning Environment (EHLE), Research Report DFE-RR142.* Available at: https://assets.publishing.service.gov.uk/media/5a75b852e5274a545822db3f/DFE-RR142a.pdf

Maslow, A.H. (1943) A theory of human motivation. *Psychological Review,* 50(4), pp. 370–396.

Mrljak, R., Arnsteg Danielsson, A., Hedov, G. and Garmy P. (2022) Effects of infant massage: A systematic review. *International Journal of Environmental Research and Public Health,* 19(11), p. 6378.

Stern D. (2018) *The Interpersonal World of the Infant: A View from Psychoanalysis and Developmental Psychology.* Abingdon: Routledge.

6

BUILDING RELATIONAL PRACTICE

AIMS OF THE CHAPTER

1. To understand the importance of keeping relationships central in our practice.
2. To support children's behaviour through love and nurture.
3. To link to the six principles of nurture.
4. To explore how we can nurture self-regulation in our children.

KEY DEFINITIONS

Listed below are the key definitions that this chapter will cover.

Relational practice	When we adopt an approach which places relationships at the heart of everything, including promoting behaviour for learning.
Self-regulation	An overarching term describing both emotional regulation (regaining feelings of calm when faced with overpowering emotions) and cognitive regulation (executive functioning skills).
Co-regulation	When adults nurture children and support them by being attuned to their emotional states and teaching them strategies, tools and calming techniques in order to help them develop self-regulation.
Emotion coaching	A method of co-regulation when we empathise, validate feelings and coach the child in the moment so they learn appropriate ways of responding to feelings and emotions.
Nurture group	A school-based small group intervention in mainstream education to support children with social, emotional and/or behavioural difficulties. Based on the principles of nurture (Lucas et al., 2006) and prioritising relationships between children, adults and peers.

INTRODUCTION

Humans are pre-programmed or hard-wired to be in relationship with each other and are social beings from birth (Bowlby, 1988). As Read so eloquently shares, 'We now know due to advances and research on brain development that the key building blocks for emotional wellbeing, good mental health and future success in life are developed through close, loving and intimate relationships' (2014, p. 3). These relationships are at the heart of a loving pedagogy, which could be described as a relational approach.

Relational practice has its roots in attachment theory and believes behaviour to be a method by which children communicate their needs. Bowlby defines attachment as 'seeking and maintaining proximity to another individual' (1969, p. 194) and attachment theory acknowledges the importance of these relationships, particularly the emotional bonds children develop with their primary caregivers, and notes the impact this can have on future relationships. Children usually return to their main carer when worried, fearful or unsure. We can see attachment theory in daily practice within settings and schools as early childhood professionals build close relationships with their children, often acting as a key person, and work closely with families, recognising that their early relationships are key to their future success. We also want our settings and schools to become secure bases for our children so that they offer emotional support and enable our children to feel safe and ready to learn.

This chapter will explore the benefits of adopting a relational approach in our settings and schools. It will particularly focus on the impact this has on supporting children's behaviour. It considers what we mean by good behaviour and explains how the most loving and nurturing approach is achieved through prioritising relationships. This chapter will also explore several strategies that could form part of a relational approach, including nurture groups, emotion coaching and co-regulation.

THE IMPORTANCE OF RELATIONSHIPS

A wealth of research highlights the importance of relationships (Gerhardt, 2015; Music, 2017; Zeedyk, 2013). Through relationships we learn empathy, social etiquette, how to relate to others and how to be a good friend. It is also through developing relationships with others we learn more about ourselves. Relationships are reciprocal and social – we cannot be in a relationship on our own and we cannot learn to self-regulate without being in relationships. 'Children are growing up in a social world and their lives are intertwined with others, therefore it would be impossible for children to self-regulate without learning alongside others' (Grimmer and Geens, 2022, p. 139).

When we are in a relationship with others, we want to spend time with them and we want them to notice us. When we are noticed, we feel valued, appreciated and seen. For example, if my colleague remembers that I was going to visit a friend in hospital at the weekend and on Monday they ask, 'How was your friend – did you manage to visit them?' you feel touched that they remembered this detail about your life. On the other hand, if you had gone to a hospital appointment yourself and your colleagues knew, then on your return to work, no one asked you how you were or how the appointment went, you might feel a little hurt, disappointed and perhaps doubt how much they care.

It is the same for children. They want to feel noticed and seen. When a child doesn't feel noticed, they might doubt your love or wonder if you care about them. Some children will question this by behaving in attention-seeking ways. Thinking about behaviour as communication reminds us that attention-seeking behaviour is actually a child clearly communicating that their emotional cup is empty (see Chapter 4) and they need more attention. They are saying, 'Please notice me. Do you love me?' through their behaviour. Rebecca Brooks suggests we view this as 'attachment-seeking' rather than 'attention-seeking' because the latter generally has negative connotations (2020).

Relationships with children are at the very heart of early childhood practice and, as earlier chapters have explored, adopting a loving and nurturing approach forms the bedrock on which everything else is built. These loving relationships give them the best possible start in life. Nicki Henderson and Hilary Smith sum this up, 'Put simply, children who are loved do better, in school and in later life' (2022).

SUPPORTING CHILDREN'S BEHAVIOUR THROUGH LOVE AND NURTURE

A relational approach is particularly significant when we consider supporting children's behaviour. This approach is counter to behaviourism which sees all behaviours as learnt through interactions with others and the environment and believes children can be trained or conditioned to behave in particular ways through reinforcement of those behaviours. Learnt behaviours may well account for a small aspect of children's behaviour; however, there is often a bigger picture to consider. Behaviourism tends to use sanctions, rewards and punishments as a way to manage children's behaviour and teach them how to behave differently. The problem with this more traditional approach is that it doesn't consider why children are behaving that way in the first place. It ignores the role emotions play in our behavioural responses and does not seek to teach any moral understanding to the child. The focus is usually on short-term obedience to rules and compliance with adult requests.

In contrast to this, a relational approach recognises the emotions underpinning the behaviour, seeks to understand why the child might be behaving this way, with the longer-term aim of teaching children right from wrong, how to respond when overwhelmed with emotions and how to be empathetic towards others. Nurture is a great word to use in relation to behaviour because we want to nurture a moral understanding in our children so that they know right from wrong and why, and are able to make moral choices and decisions.

When a child is learning to write their name and they make a mistake, we don't tell them they're wrong or insist the child has time out until they can write it properly – we nurture the child giving them plenty of opportunities to write. We role model and scaffold their learning and encourage them to try again. We also celebrate with them the small steps of progress they make along the way, for example, when they form a letter correctly, and celebrate again when they finally achieve their goal of writing their whole name. However, for some reason with behavioural mistakes the adult response is often different. We chastise the behaviour, respond harshly, give the child time out or worse, put them in isolation and insist they do better next time. Young children are learning to behave just like they're learning to read or write and we should treat this behavioural learning in the same way as we do other learning, and nurture them through the process, celebrating achievements along the way.

Adopting a relational approach reminds us to consider connection before correction (Hughes, 2009). If we have a good relationship with our children (connection), we will be better placed to help support with any behavioural mistakes (correction). A loving pedagogy nurtures children's behaviour and sees it as a child learning to develop self-regulation. It also sees all behaviour as communication. We need to work out what the child is communicating to us through their behaviour and seek to understand their needs. Then we can begin to address these and be more proactive and specific in how we support each child. In my book, *Supporting Behaviour and Emotions,* I, Tamsin, talk about becoming a behaviour detective and asking ourselves several questions to try and unpick why a child is behaving the way they are (Grimmer, 2022).

REFLECTIVE PRACTICE EXERCISE

Think about a child whose behaviour you are struggling to understand. Consider the following questions, then reflect upon what the behaviour is communicating to you and plan future provision, interactions and interventions in the light of this.

- Have their basic needs been met, for example, is the child hungry or tired?
- What is the child trying to tell me?
- Is this child communicating something with us through the way they behave? (either consciously or not)
- Why do they do what they do?
- Could this behaviour be evidence of a schema (repetitive play)?
- Could they be attention/attachment seeking?
- Does their emotional cup need refilling?
- Do they enjoy behaving that way?
- Do they like my response?
- Are they frustrated or feeling misunderstood?
- What is this child hoping to achieve through this behaviour?
- Has this behaviour been triggered by anything?
- What happened prior to this child behaving in this way?
- Has anything different happened at home?
- Is this behaviour a result of social interaction?
- Can we try to unpick why this child has acted or reacted in this way?

(Grimmer 2022, p. 73)

THROW AWAY YOUR BEHAVIOUR MANAGEMENT POLICY!

Schools and settings need to move away from seeing behaviour as something to be 'managed' and instead focus on adopting a relational approach (Grimmer, 2022; Grimmer and Geens, 2022). Several settings and schools have discarded their behaviour management policies in exchange for policies entitled, Relational Practice Policy, Relationships Policy and (Tamsin's favourite) a Loving Pedagogy Policy! This is moving away from the narrative of controlling children and seeking for them to comply with adults' requests and moving towards teaching self-regulation, moral awareness and nurturing children's learning and development through a loving approach. A relational approach does not rely on strategies involving punishment, shame or blame and is based on research which highlights the importance of being attachment and trauma-aware (discussed in Chapter 2).

In addition, research has shown that certain groups of children are more vulnerable when it comes to behaviour management and policies on punishment with the final outcome of exclusion negatively impacting our most vulnerable, for example, children with special educational needs and disabilities, those from poorest backgrounds and ethnic minorities (Gomez et al., 2021; Timpson, 2019). The majority of schools would say they strive to avoid permanent exclusion; however, using isolation as a key strategy to support behaviour is an internal exclusion described in different terms, and this practice is rife, albeit under a different name. Although isolation is used with older pupils, many early childhood professionals will enforce a type of isolation on a younger child, removing them from a group, removing privileges, secluding them from others or giving the child time-out. This is using time-out not as space and time to recover because they are dysregulated, but as a punishment for not conforming. Research shows that isolation or seclusion has a negative impact on children, creating 'docile subjects', and is a result of 'children being moulded and manipulated' (Barker et al., 2010, p. 382).

As Chapter 2 has explored, research has shown that Adverse Childhood Experiences can have a very negative impact on children's lives, affecting physical health and wellbeing and sometimes resulting in challenging behaviour. As early childhood professionals, we must seek to understand children's behaviour and, if the child has been angry or upset, look to restore their relationship with us. A relational approach is a non-judgemental approach which does not blame and shame children and is also restorative. Research in Bristol schools demonstrated that adopting a restorative approach can increase attendance, reduce fixed term exclusions, improve communication and relationships between staff and children and between children and their peers and remove the need for punishment and punitive policies (Skinns et al., 2009).

Sadly, there are some schools and settings which use behaviour management systems that publicly shame and humiliate children whilst trying to seek them to conform. For example, they may have a traffic light system, whereby each child's name is placed on the colour that best represents their behaviour, or how well they are keeping the class rules. Red means they have broken the rules, amber means they have been warned and green means they are doing well. There are many variations of these behaviour systems, such as sunshine, cloud, rainbow or smiley face, sad face, etc., and there should be no place for them within early childhood or primary education. When children are publicly shamed, it can lead to an amygdala hijack (Goleman, 1996) or the downstairs brain taking control (Siegel and Bryson, 2012), which triggers the child's freeze, fight or flight response and makes it extremely difficult for them to make the 'choice' to work quietly or conform.

Research shows that when a child is viewed negatively by others and externally shamed, this can contribute to depression and non-suicidal self-injury (Xavier et al., 2016). There is a wealth of research that shows that shaming does not prevent future misbehaviour or encourage remorse and, in fact, exacerbates the situation, is ineffective and often promotes anger and defensiveness (Goodman, 2017; Tangney, 2015). In addition, there are many children who live in the fear of these systems and go to school terrified that they will be 'put on the raincloud' or 'sad face'. We do not understand when so much is known and understood about childhood trauma and the impact of fear and cortisol on children's developing brains, why these outdated systems still exist in our classrooms and settings. A loving nurturing approach should mean we practise forgiveness as we remain non-judgemental with our children, offering them a fresh start every day.

WHAT RELATIONAL PRACTICE IS NOT. . .

Some people suggest that relational practice is wishy-washy and does not offer the children any boundaries. This is not true because it is possible to be fair and firm without needing to resort to sanctions and draconian punishments. Children thrive within consistent routines, and when they understand the rules and boundaries within a setting, it helps them to feel more safe and secure. Another critique of relational practice is the misconception that adults know better and should remain in charge at all times. Of course, adults know the bigger picture, and have overall responsibility, but does relinquishing some power to children feel threatening to certain adults? Perhaps they are afraid of what might happen if they allowed the children some autonomy or say in matters? Offering children and young people agency is about taking their views and opinions seriously and knowing, not only that they have a voice but also that using it might result in action. Our youngest children live in a world where they have very little say about many aspects of their lives. Adults decide where they go, when they go, what they eat and what they wear. They even decide what they play with a lot of the time. Children learn to be independent by being allowed to make decisions and being offered choices. This links very well with the United Nations Convention on the Rights of the Child and Article 12 in particular, which states that children should have a say in all matters affecting them and have their views taken into consideration (UNICEF, 1989).

Another counter argument claims that seeing behaviour as communication excuses the behaviour. This is a total misunderstanding of what a relational approach is about, because rather than excusing the behaviour, we are seeking to understand why a child is behaving that way. It is possible to understand behaviour without condoning it. Within a relational approach, children are encouraged to take responsibility for their actions, but they are not blamed. When overwhelmed with emotion, they are given clear boundaries about how to behave, act and react, whilst their emotions are accepted. For example, if a child is so angry that they are lashing out and hitting others, their anger would be acknowledged but their response challenged, 'It's OK to feel angry, I would feel angry if Harry took my toy, but it's not OK to hit Harry. When I feel angry I sometimes need to release the anger, so you could run outside or stamp your feet if it would help'. Later, we would also try to restore the relationship between the child and Harry and between them and us.

Understanding a child's behaviour can also help us to choose the best strategy to use when supporting them to behave differently. For example, if Sarah often chases Ryan and pinches his arm, an adult might tell Sarah off, perhaps even saying 'if you chase and pinch Ryan again you will not be allowed to play with the iPad'. The adult may have dealt with this in the short term, but they haven't helped Sarah learn how to behave instead. This response is reactive not proactive and preventative. If we seek to understand why Sarah chases and pinches Ryan, we might realise she does this because she likes him and wants him to play with her. Therefore, we can teach Sarah how to hold her hand out to Ryan or teach her a phrase to repeat asking him to play. In this way, we can avoid Sarah feeling like she needs to chase and pinch Ryan and thus avoid future conflict.

REFLECTIVE PRACTICE EXERCISE

Think about your setting/school policies, in particular the policy which discusses behaviour.

Does the title of the policy adequately describe the content?
What is the rationale for the policy?
Does it focus on 'managing' children's behaviour or seek to understand and respond sensitively to the behaviour?
To what extent does the policy promote relationships?
How do you respond to challenging behaviour? What strategies do you use? Are they preventative or reactive? Are they outlined and summarised in the policy?
How might your setting's policy become more nurturing and loving?

EMOTION COACHING

An important aspect of relational practice is enabling children to be more emotionally literate and a key way to support children to understand their emotions is to acknowledge and label them yourself. When you are sad, tell the children you feel sad and why, when you are angry, explain that you are angry and why. In this way, we are role modelling our emotional experiences and teaching children that having feelings is part of being human. Children need to understand that there are no good or bad emotions as such, all emotional responses are valid – however, how children may respond when they feel a certain way may or may not be OK (Gilbert et al., 2021). This idea fits within an emotion coaching response which emphasises the importance of looking at the emotions that underlie particular behaviours (Gottman et al., 1996) (see Figure 6.1).

Emotion coaching responds to children in the moment and is a method of co-regulation when the adult supports a child with how to deal with their emotions and teaches them strategies of how to resolve conflict, solve problems or what to do in the future if they feel this way again. For example, if we see Zenab lashing out because another child, Ezra, took their toy, an emotion coaching approach responds with empathy and guidance by saying, 'You look angry because Ezra took your toy. It's OK to feel angry, but it's not OK to hit others when you are angry. Can we think of another way of showing Ezra that you're upset?' At the same time, we would also talk to Ezra saying, 'Ezra, I can see you really wanted to play with the toy that Zenab had, I think that's why you took it from her. It's OK to want to play with the same toy, but not OK to take Zenab's toy. What could we do instead?'

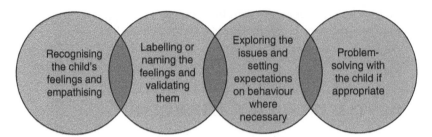

Figure 6.1 Emotion coaching in practice
Source: Gottman et al. (1996).

Emotion coaching sets limits, expectations and boundaries for children, helping them to know the rules and social etiquette involved in being a friend and playing with others. It also encourages children to 'own' any disputes and problem-solve solutions. This is very empowering and, over time, children learn how to resolve conflicts and problems amicably without always needing adult intervention. It also teaches children how to respond when they have big emotions or overwhelming feelings and helps them to self-regulate.

CASE STUDY

Joe is 4 years old and he is in the preschool room at a nursery. Joe is showing his anger by throwing his toys at the glass door; he is cross as he cannot go outside into the nursery garden to play yet. The following steps demonstrate how the early years practitioner used emotion coaching to support him.

Emotion Coaching Step 1

Tune in and reflect on the child's feelings – what are they experiencing right now, put yourself in their shoes, how does that make you feel?

What the practitioner reflected on:

Joe really likes being outside and is feeling frustrated he cannot go to the garden yet, and he is tired today and it is hard to wait at his age.

As the adult, I feel stressed as I am trying to get the other children ready too – I need to take a deep breath and self-regulate.

Emotion Coaching Step 2

Label the child's feelings out loud to soothe the nervous system.

What the practitioner said:

(Continued)

> *I can see you are frustrated as you really want to go outside to play...*

Use validation and empathy to help the child feel seen, heard and understood.

What the practitioner said:

> *It's really hard to wait for something you really want - you love being in the garden, it's tough to be indoors while we get ready.*

The adult then encouraged Joe to engage in physical activities to help him calm down.

Emotion Coaching Step 3

Set limits and expectations on the behaviour (ONLY when he has calmed right down).

What the practitioner said:

> *I understand that you really want to play outside it makes you cross when I say we have to wait, but it's not ok to throw things as that could hurt someone.*

Emotion Coaching Step 4

Problem-solve with the child to help them learn to regulate and adapt their responses.

Practitioner's reflections:

Pause, wait and listen. Joe might have some ideas. If he needs help thinking of ideas, we could scaffold his thinking.

What the practitioner said:

> *What could you do next time you feel frustrated?' Could we get a timer and that might help us to know how long until outside time?*

> (Example shared with permission from Shana Laffy, Engage Early Years, Heartful Therapy Training and Emotion Coaching UK, 2023)

THE PRINCIPLES OF NURTURE AND NURTURE GROUPS

Nurture groups have long been established in many primary schools as an inclusive low-cost and high-impact intervention for children (Boxall and Lucas, 2010). They are described as being 'for children whose emotional, social, behavioural and cognitive learning needs cannot be met in the mainstream class' (Boxall and Lucas, 2010, p. 2) and usually involve spending part of their school day in a small group with the aim of enabling them to fully participate in their class within a year. The rationale behind these groups is that many children will have missed out on essential learning in their earliest years and they seek to support and nurture these children in order to help them fully access the national curriculum.

We may not use nurture groups in our provision; however, we can all learn from the principles that underpin them and these principles are explored in detail below.

The six principles of nurture are:

1. Children's learning is understood developmentally.
2. The classroom/setting offers a safe base.
3. The importance of nurture for the development of wellbeing.
4. Language is a vital means of communication.
5. All behaviour is communication.
6. The importance of transition in children's lives.

(Lucas et al., 2006)

PRINCIPLE 1 – CHILDREN'S LEARNING IS UNDERSTOOD DEVELOPMENTALLY

The first principle explains that children's learning should be understood developmentally. This means that we should start with the child and think about individual children and their stage of development, rather than focusing on their age. As the Early Years Foundation Stage reminds us, children develop and learn at different rates (DfE, 2024) and we need to be knowledgeable about child development, so that we will be aware if a child is not progressing typically. As early childhood professionals, we need to provide developmentally appropriate resources, activities and experiences in order to allow our children to grow. We also need to adjust our expectations and view their behaviour developmentally, remembering they are learning how to self-regulate.

PRINCIPLE 2 – THE CLASSROOM/SETTING OFFERS A SAFE BASE

This principle is talking about attachment theory and ensuring that our settings are nurturing places and spaces. Young children show a preference for particular people in their lives, usually their primary or main caregivers, and want to be close to them, relying on them when they feel worried or insecure. In this way, they are using their main carer as a safe haven or secure base. Geddes (2006) explains how, in the context of an educational setting, in the absence of their main carer, the teacher and classroom can act like a secure or safe base for the children. When children use adults in this way, they will feel more able to relax, explore and learn effectively.

PRINCIPLE 3 — THE IMPORTANCE OF NURTURE FOR THE DEVELOPMENT OF WELLBEING

The third principle highlights how a nurturing approach can help to develop children's self-esteem and wellbeing. Children need to be listened to, valued, supported and their achievements celebrated. In our schools and settings, we must prioritise children's wellbeing and actively promote their self-esteem. Therefore, it can be helpful to measure their wellbeing, so that we are aware which children might need more support. One way to do this is to use the Leuven Scale of Wellbeing and Involvement (Laevers, 2005). This measurement tool considers both wellbeing and involvement separately, offering a five-point scale for each. Early Childhood Professionals can observe their children then relate what they notice to these scales. The idea is to aim to raise levels of involvement and wellbeing, because, generally speaking, engaged children will have higher levels of wellbeing.

PRINCIPLE 4 — LANGUAGE IS A VITAL MEANS OF COMMUNICATION

The fourth principle reminds us about the importance of language and how it is a vital means of communication. However, young children are still learning language and, in addition, many children may not yet have developed the skills necessary to communicate their needs and wants in this way. If we reflect upon how we use language as a reciprocal means of communication, we can identify many communication methods that do not use spoken words, for example, facial expression, eye movement, gestures, posture, behaviour, emotions, writing, symbols and mark making to name a few. If children are struggling with language, we need to use as many different forms of communication as we can to help them to be understood whilst actively trying to develop their language skills. Using signs, gestures and pictures alongside clear speech and simple phrases will help, as will role-modelling language and using strategies such as recasting, expanding, labelling and repetition. A nurturing environment is language rich and a place where all attempts at communication are highly valued.

PRINCIPLE 5 — ALL BEHAVIOUR IS COMMUNICATION

The fifth principle of nurture is that all behaviour is communication. Thinking about behaviour in this way reminds adults that there is always a reason why a child behaves the way they do, and the adult's role is to find out what the child is trying to communicate through their behaviour. Thinking about poor behaviour as just the tip of the iceberg can help us to become behaviour detectives to look beneath the surface (Grimmer, 2022).

PRINCIPLE 6 — THE IMPORTANCE OF TRANSITION IN CHILDREN'S LIVES

The last principle highlights the importance of transition in children's lives and helps the adults to be aware of this. Daly et al. (2004) remind us that children may find seemingly insignificant or trivial things stressful or even traumatic and it would be easy for us to underestimate their impact. We need to see the world and our provision through our children's eyes and try to understand how they will feel and what will affect them most. Transitions can be regarded as vertical (joining a setting, moving between settings or starting school) or horizontal (within the day or normal routine, changing rooms or moving from one part of our routine to another such as free play to tidy up time) and all need to be planned for and managed (Kagan and Neuman, 1998). One of the ways to support successful transitions is building effective relationships and getting to know the children and families well. So, adopting a relational approach and focusing on continuity rather than change is key. Allowing children to have a voice in relation to transition is also important (Mainstone-Cotton, 2020) and a helpful way of nurturing children through any change they experience.

REFLECTIVE PRACTICE EXERCISE

Reflect upon the six principles of nurture and the extent to which your practice is informed by them.

What are you doing well?
What might you stop or start doing in the light of this?
Is there anything you might do differently in the future?

CONCLUSION

Rather than viewing children's behaviour as something we need to discipline and control, we might find it helpful to instead think about nurturing children's self-regulation through relational practice. As Paul Dix explains, when the adults change their practices, everything changes (2017)! By becoming a co-regulator, we can use emotion coaching and restorative practices to support children and teach them skills such as conflict resolution, problem-solving and resilience. Part of this process is being an effective role model who responds with a calm attitude and teaches children appropriate emotional responses whilst having realistic expectations of behaviour. A relational approach also reframes 'attention-seeking' behaviour to 'attachment-seeking', highlighting the needs of the child. Adults need to be sensitive to these needs, aware of what their behaviour could be communicating and avoid using any praise or reward systems that judge children or rely on shame, humiliation or social compliance.

Ultimately, we need to ask the question – what are we aiming for in the longer term through discipline and supporting behaviour? Do we want obedient, compliant children who conform without question to authority? Or do we want self-regulated learners who are empathetic, engaged, happy, resilient and well-adjusted, who know right from wrong and are sensitive to others?

Noddings questions the traditional role of education and suggests we revise what education is aiming for, 'Our aim should be to encourage the growth of competent, caring, loving and lovable people' (1992, p. xiv). If adults who care is our destination, adopting a loving pedagogy which nurtures children is the starting point and focusing on relationships and relational practice is the route or the way we get there!

KEY QUESTIONS

To what extent could your approach be described as a relational approach?
What opportunities are there for you to use emotion coaching techniques in your practice?
What are you aiming for in the longer term through discipline and supporting behaviour?
In the light of this chapter, how can your responses to behaviour become more nurturing and loving?

Further reading and resources

Dix, P. (2017) *When the Adults Change, Everything Changes: Seismic shifts in school behaviour.* Independent Thinking Press. Emotion Coaching UK https://www.emotioncoachinguk.com/

Gilbert, L., Gus, L. and Rose, J. (2021) *Emotion Coaching with Children and Young People in Schools: Promoting Positive Behaviour, Wellbeing and Resilience.* London: Jessica Kingsley.

Grimmer, T. and Geens, W. (2022) *Nurturing Self-regulation in Early Childhood: Adopting an Ethos and Approach.* Abingdon: Routledge

Henderson, N. and Smith, H. (2022) *Relationship-based Pedagogy in Primary Schools: Learning with Love.* Abingdon: Routledge.

References

Barker, J., Alldred, P., Watts, M. and Dodman, H. (2010) Pupils or Prisoners? Institutional geographies and internal exclusion in UK secondary schools. *Area,* 42(3), pp. 378–386.

Bowlby, J. (1969) *Attachment and Loss: Volume 1. Attachment.* New York, NY: Basic Books.

Bowlby, J. (1988) *A Secure Base: Clinical Applications of Attachment Theory.* London: Routledge.

Boxall, M. and Lucas, S. (2010) *Nurture Groups in Schools: Principles and Practice.* London: SAGE.

Brooks, R. (2020) *The Trauma and Attachment Aware Classroom.* London: Jessica Kingsley Publishers.

Daly, M., Byers, E. and Taylor, W. (2004) *Early Years Management in Practice.* Oxford: Heinemann.

Department for Education (DfE) (2024) *Statutory Framework for the Early Years Foundation Stage.* Available at: https://www.gov.uk/government/publications/early-years-foundation-stage-framework--2

Dix, P. (2017) *When the Adults Change, Everything Changes: Seismic Shifts in School Behaviour.* Independent Thinking Press. Available at: https://www.emotioncoachinguk.com/

Geddes, H. (2006) *Attachment in the Classroom: The Links between Children's Early Experience, Emotional Well-Being and Performance in School.* London: Worth Publishing.

Gerhardt, S. (2015) *Why Love Matters: How Affection Shapes a Baby's Brain* (2nd edn.). Hove: Routledge.

Gilbert, L., Gus, L. and Rose, J. (2021) *Emotion Coaching with Children and Young People in Schools: Promoting Positive Behavior, Wellbeing and Resilience.* London: Jessica Kingsley.

Goleman, D. (1996) *Emotional Intelligence: Why It Can Matter More than IQ.* London: Bloomsbury.

Gomez, J., Rucinski, C. and Higgins-D'Alessandro, A. (2021) Promising pathways from school restorative practices to educational equity. *Journal of Moral Education,* 50(4), pp. 452–470.

Goodman, J. F. (2017) The shame of shaming. *Phi Delta Kappan,* 99(2), pp. 26–31.

Gottman, J., Katz, L. and Hooven, C. (1996) Parental meta-emotion philosophy and the emotional life of families: Theoretical models and preliminary data. *Journal of Family Psychology,* 10(3), pp. 243–268.

Grimmer, T. (2022) *Supporting Behaviour and Emotions in the Early Years: Strategies and Ideas for Early Years Educators.* Abingdon: Routledge.

Grimmer, T. and Geens, W. (2022) *Nurturing Self-Regulation in Early Childhood: Adopting an Ethos and Approach.* Abingdon: Routledge.

Henderson, N. and Smith, H. (2022) *Relationship-based Pedagogy in Primary Schools: Learning with Love.* Abingdon: Routledge.

Hughes, D. (2009) *Attachment Focused Parenting – Effective Strategies to Care for Children.* New York, NY: Norton.

Kagan, S. and Neuman, M. (1998) Lessons from three decades of transition research. *The Elementary School Journal,* 98(4), pp. 365–379.

Laevers, F. (2005) *Well-Being and Involvement in Care Settings: A Process-Oriented Self-Evaluation Instrument.* Leuven: Kind and Gezin and Research Centre for Experiential Education.

Lucas, S., Insley, K. and Buckland, G. (2006) *Nurture Group Principles and Curriculum Guidelines: Helping Children to Achieve.* London: Nurture Group Network.

Mainstone-Cotton, S. (2020) *Supporting Young Children through Change and Everyday Transitions: Practical Strategies for Practitioners and Parents.* London: Jessica Kingsley.

Music, G. (2017) *Nurturing Natures: Attachment and Children's Emotional, Sociocultural and Brain Development.* Abingdon: Routledge.

Noddings, N. (1992) *The Challenge to Care in Schools: An Alternative Approach to Education.* New York, NY: Teachers College Press.

Read, V. (2014) *Developing Attachment in Early Years Settings: Nurturing Secure Relationships from Birth to Five Years* (2nd edn.). Abingdon: Routledge.

Siegel, D. and Bryson, T. (2012) *The Whole-Brain Child: 12 Proven Strategies to Nurture Your Child's Developing Mind.* London: Robinson.

Skinns, L., Du Rose, N. and Hough, M., (2009) *Key Findings of the Bristol RAiS Evaluation Report Commissioned by Restorative Solutions CIC.* Available at: https://restorativejustice.org.uk/sites/default/files/resources/files/Bristol%20RAiS%20key%20findings.pdf

Tangney, J. (2015) Psychology of self-conscious emotions. In Wright, J. D. (Ed.), *International Encyclopedia of the Social and Behavioral Sciences* (2nd ed., Vol. 21, pp. 475–480). Oxford: Elsevier.

Timpson, E. (2019) *Timpson Review of School Exclusion.* Crown Copyright. Available at: https://assets.pu-blishing.service.gov.uk/government/uploads/system/uploads/attachment_data/file/807862/Timpson_review.pdf

UNICEF (1989) *United Nations Convention on the Rights of the Child.* Available at: www.unicef.org.uk/Documents/Publication-pdfs/UNCRC_PRESS200910web.pdf

Xavier, A., **Gouveia, J.** and **Cunha, M.** (2016) Non-suicidal self-injury in adolescence: The role of shame, self-criticism and fear of self-compassion. *Child and Youth Care Forum.* https://doi.org/10.1007/s10566-016-9346-1

Zeedyk, S. (2013) *Sabre Tooth Tigers and Teddy Bears: The Connected Baby Guide to Understanding Attachment.* Dundee: Suzanne Zeedyk Ltd.

7

LOVING AND NURTURING ENVIRONMENTS

AIMS OF THE CHAPTER

- To understand what a loving and nurturing environment looks like.
- To ensure your early childhood environment is inclusive and accessible for all.
- To recognise how a loving and nurturing environment can empower your children.
- To adopt a loving and nurturing approach within continuous provision.

KEY DEFINITIONS

Listed below are the key definitions that this chapter will cover.

Emotional environment	This refers to a setting's atmosphere and how emotionally secure people feel within it. Inclusive, respectful relationships are at the heart of the emotional environment.
Continuous provision	This refers to the opportunities, experiences, resources and activities available and accessible to children throughout the daily routine both indoors and outdoors.
Enhanced provision	This is when we enhance our continuous provision with new opportunities, experiences, resources and activities to keep it exciting, stimulating and interesting. It can be linked to children's interests, topics, themes or core texts.
Inclusion	This refers to minimising or removing barriers to learning and supporting children to participate and be successful regardless of any specific need or difference.

Accessible	This is when all children can access opportunities, experiences, resources and activities. For example, for an early years environment to be accessible, adults will need to consider aspects such as layout of setting and storage height of resources.
Empowering	Empowering children is about acknowledging that they can be competent and confident and enabling them to feel this way. It includes ensuring children's rights are upheld and their interests protected.
Holding in mind	Read (2014) uses this term to encompass an adult's nurturing behaviour when they think about and act in the best interests of the child.

INTRODUCTION

Many years ago, Nel Noddings challenged educational practices when she suggested the need for a caring ethos in schools (1992). Despite being over 30 years since she first raised these issues, education is still lacking in care. Focus is very much on academic achievement and we test and measure things like English, maths and science. It could be argued that we value what we measure (The Children's Society, 2015); therefore, ideally we should measure attitudes and subjects that we really want to foster, such as caring, wellbeing, pro-social behaviours and self-regulation. A relational approach grounded in love, as discussed in Chapter 6, and a loving and nurturing environment could encapsulate the caring ethos that Noddings wanted educators to adopt.

The learning environment is something that we do not always associate with loving and nurturing practices. This is because the focus is rightly on relationships, attachment and interactions. However, the environment sets the scene and provides the context for these relationships. Just as the ethos of a setting underpins practice, the environment can speak volumes about our ethos. If a setting says they are inclusive and welcome everyone, but the door is always closed, the staff rarely smile and when a child with additional needs visits they focus on the problems rather than potential solutions, we could challenge their inclusivity. In the same way, if a setting says they care but they have little time to spend with families and their interactions with the children are not loving and nurturing, this ethos could be questioned.

When we consider what constitutes a loving and nurturing environment, we are challenged to reflect upon our core values, ethos and how these ideals are lived out through daily practice.

Some of the attributes of a loving, nurturing environment are listed below:

- Safe
- Welcoming
- Inclusive
- Accessible
- Emotionally enabling
- Empowering
- Calm and natural
- Holds children in mind.

This chapter seeks to explore these elements and unpick how we can enable our environment to be more loving and nurturing.

SAFE

Have you ever felt unsafe? Once, I (Tamsin) was in a taxi on holiday when I felt unsafe due to the erratic driving of the cabby and I was unable to enjoy the journey or relax until she was in a safer space and out of the cab! Feeling unsafe pushes you into freeze, fight or flight mode, when you have too much cortisol in your brain and you feel dysregulated as your brain finds it harder to think rationally and feel calm. It is vital that our children feel safe. Keeping children safe, safeguarding and child protection are our top priorities, which no one would contest. Maslow's hierarchy of needs (1943) identifies safety immediately after physiological needs like food, warmth and shelter. 'We may generalize and say that the average child in our society generally prefers a safe, orderly, predictable, organized world, which he can count on, and in which unexpected, unmanageable or other dangerous things do not happen...' (Maslow, 1943, p. 378). Thus, most of us desire stability, predictability and routine in order to feel safe and secure.

The same is true for our children; however, we need to be aware if any of our children have suffered trauma or Adverse Childhood Experiences (see Chapter 2) because this may impact how safe and secure they feel. We will also want to find out any triggers our children may have, by getting to know them really well, spending time with them and finding out about their lives. Then we can respond sensitively, avoid triggering them unnecessarily and be preventative in our approach, offering them consistent routines and set boundaries. Helping your children know you are interested in them, you like them and you understand them will add to their feelings of security.

WELCOMING

A welcoming environment is one in which children feel safe, secure, a sense of familiarity, belonging and comfort. A loving and nurturing approach should be evident from the outset as children and families feel welcome and a sense of belonging in our provision from day one. Maslow's hierarchy of needs (1943) also includes love and belonging after physiological and safety needs, highlighting the importance of feeling this way. Many early childhood settings and schools strive for their children to see them as an extended family so that they will feel 'at home'. Research investigating how children feel about belonging noted that children's friendships are important ingredients, as is the caring nature of their educators (Einarsdottir et al., 2022). In addition, adults need to actively promote a sense of belonging and can do this through building secure attachments, encouraging friendships and pro-social behaviours.

On arrival, someone should welcome children and families by name with a warm smile. The purpose of this is to let them know you are pleased to see them and to help them feel known and seen. It is also helpful to have a consistent routine, so that when families arrive they know the drill: for example, coats and bags on pegs, self-registration, choose where to play and wave goodbye to parent. Knowing where to go and what to do is part of feeling safe and secure and will add to the familiar feeling we are aiming for. In addition, through the process of developing relationships with our children and families, we need to find out details about their lives; for example, what music they enjoy listening to, their favourite foods, celebrations they take part in or names of pets and family members. Then incorporate these details into our provision when possible. Wish them *Happy Easter* or *Eid Mubarak* as appropriate, and display photos of their family, pets and creations the children have made in our rooms. Also, ask the children to help make choices about the learning environment, resources or foods served. When possible, share children's quotations and incorporate their ideas into our daily practices.

REFLECTIVE PRACTICE EXERCISE

Think about your provision. On a scale of 1–5 (with 1 being not very welcoming and 5 being as welcoming as possible), how welcoming do you think it is?

Now, if you are able, do a quick anonymous poll via email or social media, asking the same question. You could ask staff, parents, children or other stakeholders.

Discuss as a team how you can ensure your provision gets the highest rating for being welcoming.

INCLUSIVE

A loving environment is an inclusive one. This means that we work hard to ensure every child feels included, welcome and that they belong. An inclusive provider ensures that no child or family is disadvantaged because of factors like background, ethnicity, home language, faith, disability and so on. This does not happen automatically, but through actively ensuring our policies and practices are as inclusive as possible and getting to know our children and families well. Therefore, we will need to work in partnership with our children and their families and this will help us to support and include children by reflecting on and meeting their individual needs.

Another aspect of being inclusive is ensuring we use language accurately. The use of language is an emotive subject, some people have strong views about how they would like to be described. Therefore, it is always advisable to ask the individual in question. For example, an autistic person may want to be called autistic or neurodiverse, or a gay person may prefer to be called queer. It can also be as simple as asking which pronouns to use and adding preferences onto staff lists or email signatures.

Resources need to be accessible and reflect different cultures, abilities and our local communities. When looking at our resources, can we try to make the use of non-English languages part of everyday experiences for children? For example, can we buy some food packets for our home corner from a local shop which caters for a non-English population? Can families who attend share some packaging with us, so that we are including foods eaten at home to make this area more familiar to children? This is particularly helpful if we include packaging written in a language other than English.

The benefits of an inclusive environment are numerous, and some are listed below:

- Every child feels like they matter, are valued, loved and belong.
- Children feel safe and secure.
- Children have equal access to activities and resources.

- Resources reflect the children, different cultures and the local community.
- Provision contains various areas for quiet and noisy play, including places to rest and calm down.
- Children's self-esteem is fostered and they are encouraged to be independent.

The document *Birth to 5 Matters* reminds us of several key points in relation to inclusive practice and equalities (Early Years Coalition, 2021, p. 27):

- Equalities and inclusion apply to all children and families.
- Equity requires more than treating everyone the same.
- Talking about race is a first step in countering racism.
- Building awareness through first-hand experiences has lasting impact.
- Ensure children can see themselves and their families reflected in the environment.
- Focus on the child at the centre.
- Practitioners working with children with special educational needs and disabilities acknowledge and value each child, emphasising what they can do through a strength-based perspective on disability.

Ideas of how we can put this into practice include considering representation in terms of different languages, races, abilities, ages, types of families and religions; where possible, employing a diverse range of staff who reflect the local community (race, religion, gender, sexuality, languages spoken); sharing photographs of our children and families; and ensuring that books, posters, role-play, resources, etc., depict diversity. We can also include phrases and words from our children's home languages in the daily routine, for example, singing songs and nursery rhymes. In addition, we can adopt phrases from our families, for example, if we look after a French child, we might call the children to the table by saying, 'à table!' to match how they are called at home. We will also want to include books in other languages and scripts for all children to use. Dual-language books or books written in languages other than English are not exclusively for children who speak another language; they are an important part of every child's understanding of literacy and how language can be written down in symbols and letters.

We want to help children to learn positive attitudes and challenge any negative attitudes and stereotypes, for example, using puppets, persona dolls, stories and books showing black heroes or disabled kings or queens or families with same sex parents or having a visit from a male midwife or female fire fighter. Celebrating diversity all year round, not just during Black History Month, Yom Kippur, Ramadan or Diwali, will help to avoid tokenism, as will ensuring the use of modern photographs of parts of the world that are commonly stereotyped and misrepresented.

ACCESSIBLE

Linked with being inclusive, our environments need to be accessible to our children. Although it is important, this is not just about labelling resources or ensuring they are stored within reach of the children, it may also be about minimising sensory inputs, introducing alternate communication methods and staff training. If we begin with the child and consider their needs, then, holding them in mind, try to see our environment through their eyes.

REFLECTIVE PRACTICE EXERCISE

Think about your children and take some time reflecting upon the accessibility of your learning environment.

Is there anything they wouldn't be able to reach, carry, lift, see or touch?

Is there anything that could overwhelm them within a session?

Are there any times when they might not understand the routine, tasks or how to interact with the resources?

How can you enable your children to participate more fully within a session?

Accessibility can also be about our ethos of permission. If we frown upon children moving resources from one space to another, even if we never say they can't, children will pick up on our attitude. One reception class that I (Tamsin) supported had worked really hard on labelling trays and resources; however, they had forgotten to show the children around. The children did not know that resources that appeared 'put away' in boxes or trays were actually available and could be taken out whenever they wanted to. For this class, it was a simple solution – the adults needed to talk to the children about their environment and the resources within it and take new children on a tour of the classroom showing them how to access all areas. We must ensure adults model an ethos of permission by enabling participation and encouraging children to access resources and materials independently.

EMOTIONALLY ENABLING

A loving and nurturing environment is one that is emotionally enabling, that is, it allows children to express their emotions, whilst validating and accepting them. In this way, we are respecting children's feelings and giving a clear message that all emotions are part of being human. Children are finding out about their emotions and learning how to respond when they feel certain ways. Therefore, adults need to provide an emotionally literate environment with activities and opportunities that support children to recognise and articulate their feelings and emotions. Adults should also role model using emotion language and emotion coaching techniques, for example, saying, 'When I feel cross, I sometimes go for a run. I wonder if running outside would help you too... We could go together?'

When early childhood professionals are predictable, fair and consistent in the way they respond to children, it enables children to feel secure. Part of this is providing a routine in which the children are aware of all expectations and feel like they belong, as mentioned above. For example, knowing where a child puts their bag when they arrive or understanding what the routine is when their key person changes their nappy. Again, this relies upon strong, authentic relationships being built with children and families, so having a robust key person system that moves beyond simply being organisational is helpful.

Allowing the children to express their emotions, including their love for us is really important. Thus, it is helpful to think through what we will do if a child says they love us and how we will respond as Chapter 4 has explored. The important aspect here is ensuring our response and environment enables the children to express themselves accurately and validates these emotions.

EMPOWERING

As I (Tamsin) noted in *Developing a Loving Pedagogy*,

> ...a huge advantage to developing a loving pedagogy is the way that it can empower children and enable them to feel less powerless. In adopting a loving pedagogy educators take time to become attuned to children and remain sensitive to their needs. This in turn enables children to feel understood and offers them agency and a voice. Thus feeling loved leads to feeling safe and secure which empowers children and enables them to be ready to learn and have higher levels of wellbeing.
>
> (Grimmer, 2021, p. 106)

The empowering nature of a loving pedagogy should not be underestimated. Children are generally living in an adult-centric world, where they have very little power; however, according to Prilleltensky et al. (2001), this powerlessness is largely un-researched, perhaps due to the assumptions made that, being dependants, children will have very little power or control. Yet, as early childhood professionals, we believe empowering children to be valuable and worthwhile. This will help to build their self-esteem, give them feelings of self-worth and nurture confidence and resilience, which will, in turn, equip them to cope with any future challenges.

There are many ways that we can empower children within our practice and one avenue is explored in detail by Dr Natalie Canning (Canning, 2020) as she considers the opportunities that social play provides for children to feel empowered. Her framework shared below can be used as a tool to help us reflect upon children's play and question the child in relation to their participation, ownership and voice within the play. In her occasional paper for TACTYC, Natalie shares how the framework can be used and gives the example of when the educators filmed Michael who is involved in a stick fight. They then revisit the video footage and use the framework to unpick and understand Michael's play and create a picture of empowerment for Michael.

EMPOWERMENT FRAMEWORK, DR NATALIE CANNING

The Empowerment Framework is a tool that can be used in practice to recognise and celebrate how children are negotiating their relationships with

(Continued)

peers, expressing their choices, curiosity and creativity and meaning making from different situations. Everyday play opportunities are sometimes over-looked because they are seen as regular activities but focusing on what is empowering about those interactions, and perhaps insignificant play moments, opens a door to understanding children's social interactions and experiences, how they respond and how they empower themselves through their decisions and actions.

Participation, Ownership and Voice are the three super themes of the Empowerment Framework; however, children do not have to exhibit all three of these to be empowered. The narrative that children are demonstrating through their play is significant to the process of empowerment. Therefore, it is important to consider the subthemes of the framework: how children are motivated, coordinating themselves, problem solving or using their imagi-nation and how they are empathetic towards others. The Empowerment Framework offers prompt questions to record children's play that focus on their participation, how they choose to use their voice and the way they own their play space. The answers to these questions build a layered picture of children's empowerment.

Thinking about empowerment provides opportunities to reflect and acknowledge rich learning and development that happens within children's play and how that contributes to building experiences, curiosity, interests and confidence. Empowering experiences enable children to approach chal-lenges in a positive way, with a 'can-do' attitude, a skill that is significant for adolescence and adulthood.

The Empowerment Framework is available through the Interactive Learning Diary app where video, photos and family contributions can support the documentation of empowering experiences that support children's learning. The framework provides opportunities for sharing moments important to children and the significant adults around them. It enables different points of view to be expressed, valued and recognised. The Empowerment Framework is holistic, inclusive and supportive of children's navigation through the new and exciting experiences they encounter at home, in their community and in learning environments (Figure 7.1).

Links to further information about the empowerment framework can be found in Chapter 8.

Participation
- Where is the child positioning themselves with the play?
- How is the child negotiating with others?
- How is the child taking part in the play?
- What choices or decisions is the child making to be involved in the play?

Coordination
- How are the child's movements reflecting their emotional state?
- How is the child showing their capacity to adapt?

Ownership
- How is the child showing their familiarity with the play environment?
- How is the child embracing play?
- What is the child's vested interest in the play?
- What are the commonalities between the children?
- How is the child in control of the play?
- How is the child working together with other children?

Motivation
- How is the child actively involved?
- How does the child maintain their play?

Children's Empowerment in Play

Problem solving
- How is the child communicating with others to articulate their ideas?
- In what ways is the child showing a creative response in the play situation?

Imagination
- How is the child using resources imaginatively?
- How is the child acting out their ideas?

Empathy
- How does the child support other children emotionally and physically?
- How does the child show their feelings?

Voice
- How is the child expressing their views?
- How is the child showing their preferences?
- What are the circumstances when a child is being listened to by his/her peers?

Figure 7.1 Empowerment framework with prompt questions to guide educator observations

CALM AND NATURAL

Offering children calm areas and spaces where they can relax is an important aspect of nurture. Everyone needs to recharge their batteries at times and many people feel a sense of calm within nature or natural spaces. In her book *A Sense of Place*, Annie Davy discusses how being outside and connecting with nature is key to young children's learning and wellbeing (2019). Therefore, we need to think about how calm and nurturing our spaces are – are they offering children the opportunity to self-regulate, feel calm or simply be? Do they make use of natural materials? Do we have access to calm areas inside and outside? Many settings offer access to natural areas, calming resources and mindfulness activities and create low arousal environments to ensure children are not triggered by what they provide. A natural way to nurture is perhaps to enhance our links with the outdoors and nature.

I (Tamsin) heard about a city toddler who, growing up in London, had not seen an apple tree before – let alone an orchard. His mum took him to visit an orchard and he saw apples growing on a tree for the first time. He remarked, 'Mummy, why did someone stick all those apples in the trees?' This may make us laugh or smile at his innocent naivety; however, it highlights a more serious issue that modern society is being faced with: the disconnect between children and nature. The National Trust acknowledged this concern in their *Natural Childhood* report, where they noted that, 'One in three [children] could not identify a magpie; half could not tell the difference between a bee and a wasp; yet nine out of ten could recognise a Dalek' (2012, p. 5).

The term 'Nature-Deficit Disorder' was coined by Richard Louv in his controversial book, *Last Child in the* Woods (2010). Despite its name, this is not a medical diagnosis; rather, he uses this term as a metaphor to describe the children of this generation who are, quite literally, deprived of nature and the freedom to play outdoors. He suggests that these children are more likely to have physical and emotional illnesses as a direct result of not playing outside or being connected with nature.

In addition, children in the United Kingdom are spending more and more time inside, with recent statistics suggesting that children aged between 3 and 4 spend an average of 12.7 hours per week watching television and a further 4.7 hours per week gaming online (statista.com). On top of this, a research analysis of physical activity in 2- to 4-year-olds in England found that 88.9% of children do not meet the government-recommended 180 minutes of daily physical activity (Tinner et al., 2019). With the decline in children playing outside, it is easy to see why Richard Louv is concerned and, in fact, why we all should be. It could be argued that a loving approach is one which nurtures children within nature.

HOLDS CHILDREN IN MIND

Holding children in mind could be described as being child-centred and keeping each child in mind throughout our provision; for example, when activities and resources are tailored to children who attend and where children see themselves and their families reflected in displays, notices and other areas of the setting. Read (2014) uses this term to encompass an adult's nurturing behaviour when they think about and act in the best interests of the child.

A loving nurturing environment holds children in mind and is planned around specific children and their needs. I (Tamsin) describe this as part and parcel of a loving pedagogy (Grimmer, 2021). In practice, early childhood professionals tend to do this naturally because they know their children really well and think about them when they are not with them; for example, when walking with their family at the weekend, they may see a shiny conker and pick it up saying, 'Harri will love this!'

CASE STUDY (FROM A NURSERY)

In our preschool nursery class in Warrington, designing both our continuous provision and role-play with our children in mind is very important to us. For example, before our children begin with us in September, we invite their parents/carers to email us a photograph of their child enjoying the summer holidays. They could be absolutely anywhere – on a beach, in a park or even on an aeroplane! We then print these out and use them to enhance our 'holiday-themed' role-play area before they start. It is wonderful to see their

(Continued)

(Continued)

delight when they arrive and find pictures of themselves and their families displayed for all to see! We attach Velcro on the back of the photos to enable the children to hold them and move them around the role-play arch, encouraging positive interactions and providing a wonderfully natural basis from which to help them build relationships.

We also include photos and resources about different families, such as books and jigsaws, reflecting diversity and inclusivity. We have compiled our own book showing different family demographics for the children to flick through, and we display this on a hook enabling easy access. We hang from our arch photos and words familiar to our children, such as pictures of the local park, beach, tents and places they may have visited over the holidays. We provide wooden toadstools and children's camping chairs to sit on, as well as a picnic rug and basket filled with healthy play food and plates, set on fake grass. The children love to sit and relax in a calm and natural environment, surrounded by familiar images of the people they love.

We believe it is vital that children feel safe and valued and this approach nurtures our children as they begin to build friendships with peers and attachments with adults, helping develop their personal, social, emotional and communication and language skills.

CONTINUOUS PROVISION

When considering our environment, we need to think about our continuous provision and, in theory, a loving and nurturing approach should permeate throughout it. Our ethos will be reflected within our daily routine, in our interactions with children and in our environment reflecting the needs and backgrounds of our children and families.

The Reggio Emilia approach views the environment as the 'third teacher' and sees the space as educating the child, in terms of accessibility of resources, how space is used and how it mirrors the children who occupy it (Edwards et al., 2012). This, in turn, nurtures the children and empowers them. Therefore, our spaces should be planned intentionally, designing our environments to suit the children's interests, learning and what we want them to experience during their time with us. We will want to think about how the space makes us feel in terms of layout and aesthetics and consider how each area within our continuous provision nurtures the children. We can also reflect upon the love languages of our children and ensure they are represented within our continuous provision. For example, are there spaces where children can spend quality time together? Do our spaces allow children to help each other? Are there loose parts available to enable children to gift resources to each other? Are there opportunities to role model affirming words and language in all areas of practice? What might that look like in a reading space, role-play area, or messy play provision?

CASE STUDY – CONTINUOUS PROVISION

One really easy way to ensure our learning environment fully supports the needs of our children is to simply watch them play. Taking time-out from our quality interactions and teaching opportunities is not just interesting but can be extremely invaluable too. It enables us, as educators, to enhance our continuous provision, based on the needs (and wants!) of the children. Sometimes, this will mean simply bringing in additional resources or using more of the same; but sometimes it will mean introducing new play concepts/ideas or changing things around and adapting our provision. It is important to remember that just as we, the adults, differ in our interests and personalities, so will our children and that no two cohorts of children will be the same.

Early in the autumn term last year, we noticed all our outdoor waffle building blocks were being moved and carried around by a certain group of children. Through careful and intentional observation, we realised they were being used as food and plates! Our mud kitchen is situated at the wooded end of our outdoor area, so we built a smaller, wooden café area on the flags outside with a little seating area and table. We introduced play food and modelled how to take an order on a notepad. They could of course (and sometimes did!) choose to use the waffle blocks if they wanted to, but through the introduction of new resources, along with high-quality modelling and interaction, we widened and broadened the opportunities for their play, following their interests and needs.

We have learnt how to introduce new equipment and resources in creative, cost-effective ways; for example, asking our families for donations or to advertise/collect from social media. We noticed that one particular cohort was hugely interested in babies and prams… and we only had two! So, after such a plea, we were inundated and are now surrounded by babies and prams, enabling us to rotate our enrichments.

Our continuous provision is constantly changing because our children change. We adapt our learning environment following our children's interests, enhancing and tailoring it to their specific needs and often weave important festivals or national events into our provision. We have found that keeping our provision interactive, fluid and evolving really sparks the children's interests. After all, encouraging our children to learn and grow is what we are all about!

REFLECTIVE PRACTICE EXERCISE

Consider each aspect of your continuous provision in turn and ask yourself these questions:

- To what extent does this space reflect the child (interests, background, family, etc.)?
- Is the area fully accessible to all children?
- What do we intend children to learn or experience in this space?
- Why have we planned this area in this way?
- How might this space nurture our children?
- Have we thought about children's love languages within this space?
- To what extent are we utilising natural resources and embracing nature within this area?

CONCLUSION

Adopting a loving pedagogy will impact the whole of our provision, including our learning environment. This chapter has explored how we can ensure this is loving and nurturing. The key ingredients proposed were for the environment to be safe, welcoming, inclusive, accessible, emotionally enabling, empowering, calm and natural and an environment which holds children in mind. We can also ensure we tap into children's interests and fascinations within our continuous provision, considering how the space reflects our children and how we can embrace children's love languages through our early childhood environment.

KEY QUESTIONS

1. To what extent is your environment:
   - Safe?
   - Welcoming?
   - Inclusive?
   - Accessible?
   - Emotionally enabling?
   - Empowering?

(Continued)

(Continued)
- Calm and natural?
- Holding children in mind?
2. To what extent are your core values, ethos and ideals lived out in daily practice?
3. Reflect upon how your provision is experienced by everyone (children, families, staff, governing body or other stakeholders, general public). Would it be described as loving and nurturing by all? How do you know?

References

Canning, N. (2020) *The significance of children's play and empowerment: An observational tool. TACTYC,* Occasional Paper 14, pp. 1–4.

Davy, A. (2019) *A Sense of Place: Mindful Practice Outdoors.* London: Bloomsbury Publishing.

Early Years Coalition (2021) *Birth to 5 Matters.* St Albans: Early Education. Available at: https://birthto5matters.org.uk/

Edwards, C., Gandini, L. and Foreman, G. (2012). *The Hundred Languages of Children the Reggio Emilia Experience in Transformation* (3rd edn.). Santa Barbara, CA: Praeger.

Einarsdottir, J., Juutinen, J., Emilson, A., Ólafsdóttir, S., Zachrisen, B. and Meuser, S. (2022) Children's perspectives about belonging in educational settings in five European countries, *European Early Childhood Education Research Journal,* 30(3), pp. 330–343.

Grimmer, T. (2021) *Developing a Loving Pedagogy in the Early Years.* Abingdon: Routledge.

Louv, R. (2010) *Last Child in the Woods: Saving Our Children from Nature-Deficit Disorder.* Atlantic Books.

Maslow, A. H. (1943) A theory of human motivation. *Psychological Review,* 50(4), pp. 370–396.

National Trust (2012) *Natural Childhood Report.* Quote from page 5. Available at: https://nt.global.ssl.fastly.net/documents/read-our-natural-childhood-report.pdf

Noddings, N. (1992) *The Challenge to Care in Schools: An Alternative Approach to Education.* New York, NY: Teachers College Press.

Prilleltensky, I., Nelson, G. and Peirson, L. (2001) The role of power and control in children's lives: An ecological analysis of parthways toward wellness, resilience and problems. *Journal of Applied Soc. Psyvhology,* 11, pp. 143–158.

Read, V. (2014) *Developing Attachment in Early Years Settings: Nurturing Secure Relationships from Birth to Five Years* (2nd edn.). Abingdon: Routledge.

The Children's Society (2015) *The Good Childhood Report.* Available at: https://www.york.ac.uk/inst/spru/research/pdf/GCReport2015.pdf

Tinner, L., Kipping, R., White, J., Jago, R., Metcalfe, C. and Hollingworth, W. (2019) Cross-sectional analysis of physical activity in 2–4-year-olds in England with paediatric quality of life and family expenditure on physical activity. *BMC Public Health,* 19, p. 846.

8

THE THEORETICAL CONTEXT OF LOVE AND NURTURE

AIMS OF THE CHAPTER

1. To explore the key theoretical names through the book and how they have influenced love and nurture in Early Childhood Education and Care.
2. To provide an evidence base for early childhood professionals to help with future study.
3. To signpost to further reading and resources if readers want to delve deeper into any of the themes discussed.

INTRODUCTION

The purpose of this chapter is to celebrate the entire book and emphasise important components of each chapter's theoretical context. We will discuss how the key theories in the book can shape and apply to your own early childhood practices. This chapter will focus on a few elements from each chapter, so consider it a one-stop shop where we can digest what we discussed and signpost to further research and resources. It will look at the theory, link it to practice, and how it has influenced our understanding of Love and Nurture.

We will also discuss our position on Love and Nurture now, a personal montage, if you like, of what motivated us to write this book, why we feel Love and Nurture are important now and how they should be incorporated into future early childhood practices.

TAMSIN GRIMMER

My interest in love stems from two places: the pioneering work of Dr Jools Page about *Professional Love* (2008, 2011, 2014, 2018) and the work of Chapman and Campbell around *Love*

Languages (2012). My own research centred around one setting and considered how love looks in practice with very young children. A loving, nurturing approach also incorporates my other passion which is fostering self-regulation in our children. Adopting a loving pedagogy is the most nurturing approach we can take and, in my view, love and nurture are almost impossible to separate. In combining my interest in love with Aaron's interest in nurturing practices, I think we describe an approach within which all children can thrive.

AARON BRADBURY

Early childhood practice for me is all about love and nurture. In the early years, it should be at the forefront of our discussions. Sadly, play is slowly being shifted into a context of school readiness, muting holistic development such as wellbeing and belonging. In Chapter 5, there is a concept of focusing on the child right *now*. As a result of focusing on our children's mental health and wellbeing, our early years practices will be more aligned to what we believe is child-centred learning.

CHAPTER 1 – SCIENCE OF LOVE, CARE AND NURTURE IN THE EARLY YEARS

This chapter focuses on a brief discussion about science and how brain development can be supported through the concepts of love and nurture. There are several theories or pieces of research which have informed this chapter and it is quite difficult to explain a few. Nurturing the child builds upon the work of attachment theorists such as Bowlby (1988) and Ainsworth (1978). However, a number of recent researchers and academics are using science to help us better understand child development, emotional attachment and why it is crucial to nurture the human brain during the earliest years, such as Goswami (2006, 2015), Conkbayir (2017, 2023), Grimmer (2021, 2023) and Zeedyk (2013). Science and research shows that a child feels secure when they are in a relationship that fosters warmth, intimacy and happiness.

In the field of early childhood development, Usha Goswami's research is a driving force which focuses on the cognitive development and learning of children (2006; 2015). As a key driver of learning and development, Goswami places the child at the centre. Since the Plowden Report explained in 1967 that 'At the heart of the educational process lies the child', there has been an enormous amount of research into cognitive development (Plowden, 1967, p. 7). As Goswami points out, this reflects the same emphasis in 2015. Early childhood professionals are often interested in how the brain works and how it functions (Garvey, 2018). Suzanne Zeedyk is a contemporary voice in the field of early childhood education. With this book focusing on love and nurture, her discussions and research around brain development are integral. The science of neuroscience is now readily available to the general public. The availability of books from well-known early childhood researchers has made neuroscience and its application to practice much easier to understand. Regardless of the importance of brain development and its accessibility, according to Zeedyk (2018), cited in Garvey (2018), information on babies' brain development has not yet been standardised in anti-natal classes or within early childhood programmes.

So, to support the foundations of this book, we felt that the discussion around epigenetics allowed us to deepen the understanding of why the nature and the nurture aspects of the developing child supports the ongoing debate as to why love and nurture are fundamental for understanding children's holistic development. As Goswami asserts,

Genetic differences between children also influence development. However, the fact that genes influence development makes it even more important to provide optimal early learning environments for all children, so that environmental differences and genetic differences are not additive in their effects. (2015, p. 2)

Therefore, there is a need for more research and understanding of how environments and genetics are intertwined and the positive impact that love and nurture can have on child development.

Further reading and resources

The Harvard University Center on the Developing Child has an interesting infographic explaining epigenetics and how it relates to child development, available at https://developingchild.harvard.edu/resources/what-is-epigenetics-and-how-does-it-relate-to-child-development/.

CHAPTER 2 – WHAT CONSTITUTES LOVE AND NURTURE IN THE EARLY YEARS?

Tamsin's work around loving pedagogy (Grimmer, 2021, 2023) is the key theory explored in this chapter, with references to supporting theory and research such as Bronfenbrenner (1979), Read (2014) and Noddings (2002). Loving and nurturing practices are seen as interconnected and inseparable.

Children need to be loved unconditionally, which is about the adults choosing to love children regardless of their behaviour, their actions or even their feelings towards us. There is very little neuroscientific research into unconditional love (Beauregard et al., 2009). It was first studied by Sorokin in the 1950s and describes caring and engaging in acts of service towards another person without expecting anything in return. 'Unconditional love is extended to all others without exception, in an enduring and constant way. . . Undoubtedly, this type of love is paramount for the future of our world and humanity' (Beauregard et al., 2009, p. 94).

Chapter 2 also highlights the importance of being attachment-aware and trauma-responsive in our practice. This is a key element of a loving pedagogy and one which is being more widely known about, acknowledged and adopted as the research base supporting this position increases. Some multi-academy trusts, nursery groups and schools are including these values within their policies and procedures. Many are also focusing on mental health and wellbeing as society becomes more aware of these needs. Read (2014) reminds us that loving relationships form the basis for emotional wellbeing and good mental health; therefore, adopting a loving and nurturing approach will provide children with a solid foundation.

Further reading and resources

For more information about trauma-informed practice in early child development, you may want to read this document from the National Children's Bureau: https://www.ncb.org.uk/sites/default/files/uploads/attachments/ABS%20Insight%204%20-%20Trauma%20Informed%20Practice%20-%20FINAL%20lo-res.pdf

This free online course about Adverse Childhood Experiences is also worth a look: https://www.acesonlinelearning.com/

You can read more about Tamsin's work in relation to a loving pedagogy on her website. There are links to blogs, podcasts and training about this topic: https://www.tamsing-rimmer.com/loving-pedagogy

CHAPTER 3 – THE NURTURED CHILD

Chapter 3 considers nurture from the perspective of the child. Maslow (1970) reminds us about meeting children's basic needs and the importance of love and belonging. According to the researchers, children can learn about themselves in a caring and empathetic environment when there is a safe, secure and nurturing environment.

Another key message in the chapter is that nurture needs to be viewed through a holistic lens. Children are full of potential and part of our role as early childhood professionals is to help them towards achieving this potential. We cannot look at developing one area or skillset but need to view the child as a whole. This will help children to succeed both in the here and now and also set them up for the future.

The Framework for Nurturing Care mentioned in Chapter 3 suggests there are five interrelated components which are essential when encouraging young children to thrive in their earliest years. These components will now be explored in a little more detail as described in the document *A Closer Look at the Nurturing Care Components* (Nurturing Care for Early Childhood Development, 2020):

1. Good health – Refers to the health and well-being of the children and their caregivers. Why both? We know that the physical and mental health of caregivers can affect their ability to care for the child.
2. Adequate nutrition – Refers to maternal and child nutrition. Why both? We know that the nutritional status of the mother during pregnancy affects her health and wellbeing and that of her unborn child. After birth, the mother's nutritional status affects her ability to provide adequate care to her young child.
3. Safety and security – Refers to safe and secure environments for children and their families. Includes physical dangers, emotional stress, environmental risks (eg, pollution) and access to food and water.
4. Opportunities for learning – Refers to any opportunity for the baby, toddler or child to interact with a person, place or object in their environment. Recognises that every interaction (positive or negative) or absence of an interaction is contributing to the child's brain development and laying the foundation for later learning.
5. Responsive caregiving – Refers to the ability of the parent/caregiver to notice, understand and respond to their child's signals in a timely and appropriate manner. This is considered the foundational component because responsive caregivers are better able to support the other four components.

The framework offers suggestions for interventions that organisations can put in place, which will support each component; for example, to promote good health, we can offer kangaroo care for very young babies or provide information to our families about childhood diseases and immunisations. To promote adequate nutrition, we can promote healthy eating or provide healthy food, drink and snacks to our children. In relation to safety and security, we can build secure attachments and offer safe places to play. Early childhood professionals have a large part to play in offering opportunities for early learning and development through our routines, activities, curriculum and ethos, from singing every day with children to providing stimulating and engaging provocations in our learning environment. Lastly, to promote responsive care-giving, we can role model and encourage caregivers to make eye contact, smile, cuddle, praise and generally help them to notice their child's cues and respond appropriately with sensitivity and responsiveness.

Further reading and resources

The Nurturing Care Framework for Early Childhood Development was launched by the World Health Organization, UNICEF and the World Bank Group, in collaboration with the Partnership for Maternal, Newborn & Child Health and the Early Childhood Development Action Network, during the 71st World Health Assembly on 23 May 2018. On their website, there is a wealth of information relating to nurturing care and the five components mentioned in Chapter 3: https://nurturing-care.org/about/what-is-the-nurturing-care-framework/.

CHAPTER 4 – LOVE LANGUAGES AND NURTURING TOUCH

The key theory shared in Chapter 4 is around love languages. Gary Chapman wrote his first book, *The 5 love languages: The secret to love that lasts,* about this in 1992. This focused on relationships between consenting adults, for example, within a marriage or partnership. He proposed that everyone likes to give and receive love in different ways, their own love languages if you like, and his 'secret' to lasting love was speaking the love language of your partner! It makes sense if you think about it, because if someone's love language is words and their partner never says, 'I love you', it wouldn't matter how much time they spend together or how many gifts are given, without hearing those magic words, they might not feel loved. On the other hand, if someone's love language is gifts, hearing those words might not mean anything, but receiving a bouquet of flowers or tickets to see a show might demonstrate their love and carry more meaning.

Gary Chapman teamed up with Ross Campbell and in 2012 wrote the book *The 5 love languages of children* and this resonated with me (Tamsin) as I was a fairly new parent with three young children and I wondered if my children felt loved. I knew they were loved, but I wanted them to feel it. So, I tried to find out and speak their love languages. I then reflected upon the early childhood professionals working with them and thought about my own practice as a childminder and previously as a teacher. I wondered if the children I had looked after also felt loved. I did love them, but did they feel it? This, in conjunction with reading Jools Page's work around 'professional love', led me to study and I began my own research into love.

One of the love languages is touch and Chapter 4 has also considered this area in a little more detail. We share the work of Professor McGlone who is researching the two types of touch systems: discriminative and affective touch. Discriminative touch refers to when we immediately feel the sensation of touch, our first response if you like, and affective describes the slightly delayed emotional connection or the pleasant soothing feeling that the touch gives us.

McGlone believes that nurturing touch has a significant impact on the developing brain (McGlone et al., 2014).

Further reading and resources

If you want to find out more about love languages, including completing a quiz which helps you identify your own love languages, you might want to visit this website: https://5love-languages.com/.

If you are interested in digging deeper into the area of positive touch, you might want to look up Professor McGlone's work in this area. There are several YouTube videos available, but I highly recommend watching this interview by Kathie Brodie on Early Years TV: https://www.earlyyears.tv/episode/professor-francis-mcglone/.

CHAPTER 5 – LOVE AND NURTURE BEYOND THE SETTING

Bronfenbrenner's ecological systems theory (1979) is revisited as Chapter 5 reminds us that children are part of a family, wider community and society and we must ensure we are outward looking in our nurturing approach. In his theory, the child is firmly at the centre of practice and the many influences on the child are acknowledged. We believe his theory encapsulates love and nurture, as Tamsin explains,

> When we develop a loving pedagogy, we are keeping children at the heart of what we do, holding them in mind and promoting their best interests. This empowers them as they feel listened to, heard and are valued as part of our setting. It is as if in adopting a loving pedagogy we are putting Bronfenbrenner's theory into practice.
>
> (Grimmer, in Bradbury and Swailes, 2022a, p. 23)

Baby and infant massage is also shared as an example of how we can develop nurture and love through parent workshops. Research is shared, which highlights the importance of massage for bonding, mothers' mental health and wellbeing in terms of reducing anxiety and stress (Galanakis et al., 2015; Garmy, 2012; Gürol and Polat, 2012). In addition, Peter Walker shares his knowledge about the importance of parents allowing their child time to achieve developmental milestones.

Further reading and resources

If you want to delve deeper and use the ecological systems theory more in your practice, this article from the *Cambridge Educational Research e-Journal* helps us to think about promoting children's resilience and uses Bronfenbrenner's research. Antony, E. M. (2022). Framing Childhood Resilience Through Bronfenbrenner's Ecological Systems Theory: A Discussion Paper. *Cambridge Educational Research e-Journal*, 9, 244–257. Available at https://cerj.e-duc.cam.ac.uk/currentissue/v9_2022/v9_18_244-257_antony.pdf

You can read more about Peter's Baby Massage Teacher Training here: http://www.baby-massageteachertraining.com/about/.

CHAPTER 6 – BUILDING RELATIONAL PRACTICE

In order to love and nurture children, we enter into a relationship with them and their families and we need a sound understanding of attachment theory and attachment behaviours. The most effective approach to adopt is a relational one, which places relationships at the heart of our practice and lives. Chapter 6 explores the implications of adopting such an approach for behaviour and how we can nurture children through the relationships we build. It draws upon Tamsin's work around behaviour (Grimmer, 2022b) and self-regulation (Grimmer and Geens, 2022), which recognises all behaviour as communication and requires early childhood professionals to look underneath the behaviour to the needs of the child. Adults can become 'behaviour detectives' and try to work out the reasons why children behave the way they do (Grimmer, 2022b).

Golding and Hughes (2012) share the strategy PACE, which stands for Playfulness, Acceptance, Curiosity and Empathy and describes a way of interacting with children which allows them to feel safe and secure whilst responding to their behaviour. Although Golding and Hughes aim this strategy at parents, it is a useful acronym to help us respond to our children within early childhood education provision. Love is, according to Golding and Hughes, 'The essential ingredient that makes PACE work' (2012, p. 20). Therefore, it fits perfectly within a loving and nurturing approach. Let us unpick this strategy a little more. Playfulness allows us to connect with children emotionally and respond to them with humour and fun. Using a playful tone with children can allow us to address misbehaviour in a non-threatening way. Acceptance of children's feelings and emotions is an essential ingredient when supporting children and links with the way we unconditionally love them regardless of their behaviour. Curiosity is about adults wanting to know more about why children respond in particular ways, getting to know our children and what makes them tick, then using this information to interact sensitively. Lastly, responding with empathy is vital, so that our children feel understood and their feelings validated.

PACE complements the strategy of emotion coaching as this begins with empathising and then validating the children's feelings. Tamsin has used emotion coaching with children as young as 18 months old and it is a nurturing approach that fits beautifully within a loving pedagogy. Emotion coaching relies on a certain level of language understanding; however, we can simplify what we say and also use signs, gestures and pictures to further exemplify our words when working with toddlers, children with English as an additional language or children who have language delay.

Further reading and resources

Paul Dix's 2017 book, *When the Adults Change, Everything Changes*, is a great way of reflecting upon children's behaviour and the impact adults have on it.

If you want to find out more about emotion coaching, you may want to visit the Emotion Coaching UK website – https://www.emotioncoachinguk.com/ – or read the following book:

Gilbert, L., Gus, L., & Rose, J. (2021) *Emotion Coaching with Children and Young People in Schools: Promoting Positive Behaviour, Wellbeing and Resilience*. London: Jessica Kingsley.

The following document delves deeper into how we can use PACE in schools (and we would add settings): https://www.oxfordshire.gov.uk/sites/default/files/file/children-and-families/PACEforteachers.pdf

CHAPTER 7 – LOVING AND NURTURING ENVIRONMENTS

The key document shared in this chapter is the non-statutory guidance document, *Birth to 5 Matters* (Early Years Coalition, 2021). Both Aaron and Tamsin were involved with writing the section on inclusive practices and equalities based on the views from early childhood professionals collated through several public consultations. The guidance contains practical ideas of how we can put the values into practice and we have included some of these ideas in Chapter 7.

A great strength of our early years workforce is the diversity within it, as every school and setting is as different from each other as the children who attend differ from each other. This means that we need to take ownership of our own environment and consider how we can ensure it is loving and nurturing in our context and locality with our children and families. Dr Natalie Canning's Empowerment Framework (Canning, 2020) is a great tool that can help us to reflect upon our unique situation and how our loving pedagogy can empower our individual children.

The chapter also considers our environment in terms of our continuous provision and how we can hold children in mind throughout our provision. When we hold children in mind, we are attuned to their needs, we can tap into their interests and think about their love languages when planning provision. In *Developing a Loving Pedagogy*, Tamsin shares some ways that we can be attuned and hold children in mind:

- Supporting the child in the moment, responding sensitively.
- Observing and noticing things they are interested in.
- Genuinely listening and acting upon what we hear.
- Co-constructing ideas during play.
- Being fascinated by what our children are doing and wanting to find out more.
- Considering the 100 languages of children.
- Using a Mosaic approach to better understand our children.
- Interacting sensitively, with our focus on the child, not our agenda.
- Planning interventions for particular children.
- Providing specific resources based on our knowledge of the children.

(Grimmer, 2021, p. 126)

Further reading and resources

Birth to 5 Matters is a non-statutory guidance document which early years professionals in England can use to help them implement their statutory framework. Despite it being written for an English audience, it contains valuable guidance which will be helpful for all early years professionals within the United Kingdom and internationally. It is available to download or view online at https://birthto5matters.org.uk/.

Further information about the empowerment framework (Cannings, 2020) can be found at www.rightsinplay.co.uk/empowerment and https://www.interactivelearningdiary.co.uk/empowering-children/.

CONCLUDING THOUGHTS

We are all on a journey in our professional lives and continually learning as we find out more about child development and neuroscience, and use this information to reflect upon our ethos, values and practices. We hope this book has articulately shared theory and research which confirms that adopting a loving and nurturing approach is vital in our day-to-day practices. In loving and nurturing our children today, we are helping to create a more loving and nurturing society in the future. This is not a quick fix or simple solution, but an ethos that will need hard work and effort on our part and constant reflection and revisiting as we work with different children and families and changing staff teams year on year.

Just as a spark needs feeding to become a flame, we hope this book has fuelled your own loving, nurturing approach so that it will shine more brightly and its warmth will touch everyone who encounters your provision.

KEY QUESTIONS

1. Whilst reading this book, what theme or theory has particularly resonated with you?
2. How do you intend applying what you have learnt or read about in your daily practice?
3. How might you articulate your loving and nurturing approach and ensure it underpins both policy and practice?

References

Ainsworth, M. D. S. (1978) The Bowlby Ainsworth attachment theory. *Behavioural and Brain Sciences*, 1(3), pp. 436–438.

Beauregard, M., Courtemanche, J., Paquette, V., and Landry St-Pierre, E. (2009) The neural basis of unconditional love. *Psychiatry Research: Neuroimaging*, 172(2), pp. 93–98.

Bowlby, J. (1988) *A Secure Base: Clinical Applications of Attachment Theory*. London: Taylor & Francis.

Bronfenbrenner, U. (1979). *The Ecology of Human Development: Experiments by Nature and Design*. Boston, MA: Harvard University Press.

Canning, N. (2020) *The significance of children's play and empowerment: An observational tool*. TACTYC, Occasional Paper 14. pp. 1–4.

Chapman, G. (1992). *The 5 Love Languages: The Secret to Love that Lasts*. Chicago, IL: Northfield Publishing.

Chapman, G. and Campbell, R. (2012). *The 5 Love Languages of Children*. Chicago, IL: Northfield Publishing.

Conkbayir, M. (2023) *The Neuroscience of the Developing Child: Self-Regulation for Wellbeing and a Sustainable Future*. Abingdon: Routledge.

Conkbayir, M. (2017) *Early Childhood and Neuroscience: Theory, Research, and Implications for Practice*. London: Bloomsbury Publishing.

Early Years Coalition (2021) *Birth to Five Matters Non-statutory Guidance to the Early Years Foundation Stage*. Available at: https://birthto5matters.org.uk/wp-content/uploads/2021/03/Birthto5Matters-download.pdf

Galanakis, M., Ntaouti, E., Tsitsanis, G. and Chrousos, G. P. (2015). The effects of infant massage on maternal distress: A systematic review. *Psychology*, 6, p. 2091.

Garmy, P. (2012) Aktuellt Kunskapsläge Om Spädbarnsmassage -Systematisk Litteraturöversikt 2006–2011. *Vård I Nord*, 32, pp. 29–33.

Golding, K. and Hughes, D. (2012) *Creating Loving Attachments. Parenting with PACE to Nurture Confidence and Security in the Troubled Child*. London: Jessica Kingsley Publishers.

Goswami, U. (2015) *Children's Cognitive Development and Learning (CPRT Research Survey 3)*. York: Cambridge Primary Review Trust.

Goswami, U. (2006) Neuroscience and education: From research to practice? *Nature Reviews Neuroscience*, 7, pp. 406–413.

Grimmer, T. (2021) *Developing a Loving Pedagogy in the Early Years: How Love Fits with Professional Practice*. Abingdon: Routledge.

Grimmer, T. (2022a) Bronfenbrenner, chapter 2. In Bradbury, A. and Swailes, R. (Eds.), *Early Childhood Theories Today*. London: Learning Matters.

Grimmer, T. (2022b) *Supporting Behaviour and Emotions in the Early Years: Strategies and Ideas for Early Years Educators*. Abingdon: Routledge.

Grimmer, T. (2023) Is there a place for love in an early childhood setting? *Early Years*, 42(5).

Grimmer, T. and Geens, W. (2022) *Nurturing Self-Regulation in Early Childhood: Adopting an Ethos and Approach*. Abingdon: Routledge.

Gürol, A. and Polat, S. (2012) The effects of baby massage on attachment between mother and their infants. *Asian Nursing Research*, 6, 35–41.

Maslow, A. (1970) *Motivation and Personality* (2nd edn.). New York, NY: Harper and Row.

McGlone, F., Wessberg, J. and Olausson, H. (2014) Discriminative and affective touch: Sensing and feeling. *Neuron*, 82(4), pp. 737–755.

Noddings, N. (2002) *Starting at Home: Caring and Social Policy*. London: University of California Press.

Nurturing Care for Early Childhood Development (2020) *A closer look at the nurturing care components*. Available at: https://nurturing-care.org/nurturing-care-components/

Page, J. (2008) Permission to love them. In Nutbrown, C. and Page, J. (Ed.) *Working with Babies and Young Children from Birth to Three*. London: SAGE.

Page, J. (2011) Do Mothers want professional carers to love their babies? *Journal of Early Childhood Research*, 9(3), pp. 310–323.

Page, J. (2014) Developing 'professional love' in early childhood settings. In **Harrison, L.** and **Sumsion, J.** (Eds), *Lived Spaces of Infant-Toddler Education and Care – Exploring Diverse Perspectives on Theory, Research, Practice and Policy.* (Vol. 11, pp. 119–130). *International Perspectives on Early Childhood Education and Development Series.* London: Springer Publishing.

Page, J. (2018) Characterising the principles of Professional Love in early childhood care and education. *International Journal of Early Years Education*, 26(2), pp. 125–141.

Plowden, B. (1967) *Children and Their Primary Schools: A Report of the Central Advisory Council of Education England.* London: H.M.S.O.

Read, V. (2014) *Developing Attachment in Early Years Settings: Nurturing Secure Relationships from Birth to Five Years* (2nd edn.). Abingdon: Routledge.

Sorokin, P. (1950) *Exploration in Altruistic Love and Behavior: A Syposium.* Boston, BA: Beacon Press.

Zeedyk, S. (2013) *Sabre Tooth Tigers and Teddy Bears: The Connected Baby Guide to Understanding Attachment.* Dundee: Suzanne Zeedyk Ltd.

Zeedyk, S. (2018) Foreword. In **Garvey, D.** (Ed.), *Nurturing Personal, Social and Emotional Development in Early Childhood: A Practical Guide to Understanding Brain Development and Young Children's Behaviour.* London: Jessica Kingsley.

INDEX